100 THINGS TO DO IN GREENVILLE, SC BEFORE YOU DIE

Liberty Bridge
Credit Christen Clinkscales

100 THINGS TO DO IN GREENVILLE, SC BEFORE YOU DIE

STEPHANIE BURNETTE

Reedy Press
PO Box 5131
St. Louis, MO 63139, USA
reedypress.com

Library of Congress Control Number: 2025936732

ISBN: 9781681065373

Design by Jill Halpin

Cover photo courtesy of Christen Clinkscales

Unless otherwise noted, all photos are courtesy of the author or believed to be in the public domain.

Printed in the United States of America
25 26 27 28 29 5 4 3 2

DEDICATION

To my mom, with love

Canvas Mural
Credit Christen Clinkscales

CONTENTS

Acknowledgments xiii

Preface xiv

Food and Drink

1. Drink like a Local at The Community Tap 2
2. Make Cocktail Hour a Twofer at Swordfish Cocktail Club and the Rabbit Hole 3
3. Watch the Documentary *Great Wall* and Then Dine at Sum Bar 4
4. Happy Hour It Up at Coral 5
5. Order a Pomegranate Martini at Pomegranate On Main 6
6. Watch a Panoramic Sunset at Juniper 8
7. Enjoy Celebrated Brews at Fireforge Crafted Beer 10
8. Eat a Shrimp Taco at the Drop-In Store 11
9. Brunch at Fork and Plough 12
10. Indulge at LaRue Fine Chocolate 14
11. Drink the Cheapest Wine in Greenville at Northampton Wine + Dine 16
12. Inhale Tacos at Comal 864 17
13. Get Crabby at Soby's 18
14. Sit at the Chef's Counter at CAMP 19

15. Watch Main Street from Above at Jianna 20
16. Slurp Oysters at the Jones Oyster Co. 22
17. Devour a Cathead Biscuit at Maverick 23
18. Order It All at Scoundrel 24
19. Get Off the Trail at The Commons 26
20. Try Afghan Cuisine at Aryana 27
21. Book a Table for Sunday Dinner at Topsoil 28
22. Devour Crepes at Tandem 29
23. Get Some 'Que at Mike & Jeffs 30
24. Order Fried Chicken at OJ's Diner 32
25. Don't Unwrap This Bagel at Sully's Steamers 33
26. Pair a Coffee and Beer at Grateful Brew 34
27. Carb Load at Rise Bakery 35
28. Lunch with a Cause at Jasmine Kitchen 36
29. Double Down at Harry's Hoagie Shoppe and Mike's Cheesesteaks 38
30. Go Coffee Tasting at Coffee Underground and Methodical 39

Music and Entertainment

31. Kick-Start Your Weekend at Saturday Market 42
32. Buy a Ticket for Euphoria 43
33. Get Up Close to Local Artists at Art & Light Gallery 44

34. Catch a Show at Radio Room 45
35. Sing Live Band Karaoke at Smileys on the Roxx 46
36. Hang Out at the Peace Center Complex 48
37. Snap a Selfie at the Stone Mural Project 50
38. Catch a Show at a Local Theater 51
39. Experience Main Street Fridays 52
40. Sing Your Heart Out at The Well 53
41. Camp at the Albino Skunk Fest 54
42. Get Your Bard On at Shakespeare in the Park 55

Sports and Recreation

43. Catch a Ball at Fluor Field 58
44. Visit the Home of Shoeless Joe Jackson 59
45. Chip Away at 3's Greenville Golf and Grill 60
46. Get Outside at Unity Park 61
47. Hike Paris Mountain State Park 62
48. Hop on the Swamp Rabbit Trail 64
49. Mountain Bike Gateway Park 65
50. Win a Match at PKL Park 66
51. Traverse Cleveland Park 67
52. Head to Herdklotz Park 68
53. Explore a Secret Garden 69

54. Go Wild at the Greenville Zoo 70
55. Pick a Bouquet at Sassafrass Flower Farm 71
56. Fill a Bucket of Berries at Beechwood Farms 72
57. Ride the Trolley Through Downtown 74
58. Experience the Thrill of the Greenville Swamp Rabbits 76
59. Hit the Greens at Furman University 78
60. Show Your Hometown Pride with the Greenville Triumph 79
61. Cheer On the Clemson Tigers at Memorial Stadium 80
62. Bike like the Pros at Hotel Domestique 81

Culture and History

63. Stand Where the Claussen Bakery Strike Occurred 84
64. Climb the Campanile at Furman University 85
65. Experience Art in Public Places 86
66. Experience an Award-Winning Children's Museum 88
67. Go Where the Galleries Are in West Greenville 90
68. Visit a Church Full of Artists at Oyé Studios 91
69. Walk Across the Poinsett Bridge 92
70. Explore Falls Park and the Liberty Bridge 94
71. Learn Something New at the Upcountry History Museum 96
72. Take a Walk with Greenville History Tours 97
73. Stroll Historic Earle Street 98

74. Stay at The Poinsett Hotel 100

75. Find All the Mice on Main 101

76. Fall into the World of Jasper Johns at Greenville County's Art Museum 102

77. Check Out a Reimagined Textile Complex at the Taylors Mill 104

78. Go to the BMW Zentrum 105

79. Visit One of the Oldest Buildings in the Upstate at Hans & Franz 106

80. Walk the Campus of the SC Governor's School for the Arts 107

Shopping and Fashion

81. Take a Cooking Class at the Cook's Station 110

82. Step into Lilly Pulitzer HQ at Pink Bee 111

83. Unleash Your Inner Kid at O.P. Taylor's 112

84. Dress to Impress at Augusta Twenty 114

85. Experience Timeless Style and Unmatched Service at Rush Wilson 115

86. Celebrate the Handmade at Indie Craft Parade 116

87. Create Your Own Scent at Greenville Soy Candle Company 117

88. Discover Unique Treasures at Urban Digs 118

89. Shop till You Drop at the Nested Fig Home and the Nested Fig Garden 120

90. Immerse Yourself at the Grand Bohemian Gallery 122
91. Become Part of the Story at M. Judson Booksellers 124
92. Experience Thoughtful Fashion at Custard Boutique 126
93. Shop like an Insider at the Wilson Girls Pop-Up 127
94. Find Instagram-Worthy Style at Harringtons 128
95. Step Back in Time at Mast General Store 130
96. Get Ready to Get Wet at Splash on Main 132
97. Don High-End Fashion at Coleman Collection 133
98. Buy Vintage at Old Skool Outfitter 134
99. Say Yes to the Dress at the Poinsett Bride 135
100. Taste a World of Flavor at Oil & Vinegar 136

Activities by Season 137
Suggested Itineraries 139
Index 142

ACKNOWLEDGMENTS

Thank you to the City of Greenville for welcoming me so graciously. I thought I would stay for a year and now, decades later, I call it home. Thank you to Christen Clinkscales, who shot the photos for the book, including the cover, and for her extensive help on the shopping section. Thank you to my family and friends, who always seem game for an adventure, big or small. Lastly, thank you to Taryn Scher, who brought me this opportunity, and to Reedy Press for thinking I was the right one to write it.

PREFACE

The first time I visited Greenville it was raining. My fiancé and I were thinking about a move, and as we sat in the window at Trio for lunch, I recall wondering, Could this be the next great Southern town? It was picturesque, yes, and charming like a lot of small towns, but Greenville had a sparkle, even decades ago. Maybe it was the tree-lined Main Street with its sidewalks and twinkle lights. It certainly wasn't the booming retail; at the time there was more plywood covering windows than there were shops. Looking back, I think it was the warmth, and a bristling optimism that felt exciting, an anticipation of what was to come.

Lucky for us, the hunch was right. Since then, Greenville, South Carolina—or #yeahthatgreenville—has become a heralded place both in which to live and to visit. Its downtown, historic neighborhoods, industry and schools, music scene, and places to eat and drink all seem to rise to the top of national lists.

A tiny history lesson tells us that Greenville isn't very old. The Cherokee lived here, some say along the Reedy River. But colonists didn't get here for a while. It was Charlestonians escaping mosquitoes who started building here for summer homes.

It was the Industrial Revolution that turned a sleepy town into a booming seat of manufacturing. Cotton mills helped Greenville become the "Textile Capital of the World." Later, auto-related manufacturing arrived, anchored by Michelin and BMW planting their flags here.

Today, it's tech and quality of life driving economic growth, as well as tourism, which might be why you're reading this. I'm happy to report that Trio is still at the corner of Main and Coffee Streets, and for sure the spirit that attracted us remains too; it's a feeling I know you'll experience, and I hope it whispers, "Yep, you're welcome here too."

DeMarco's
Credit Christen Clinkscales

FOOD AND DRINK

1

DRINK LIKE A LOCAL
AT THE COMMUNITY TAP

Greenville's friendliest bottle shop features craft beer on tap and farm-driven wine. The staff offers geek-level advice, and there are tastings and tap takeovers too. The shop includes a wine and beer bar and outdoor covered patio seating. Locals really show up to sip and hang out, and there's nearly always a food truck parked out front. Owners Ed Buffington and Mike Okupinksi sell what they drink, hire for passion, and host events of all sizes showcasing the best of the best from beer, wine, and cider producers. Known locally as The Tap, you won't be a stranger for long. There are two other locations of The Community Tap, and they are equally special and uniquely their own. One is right on an urban walking path called the Swamp Rabbit Trail, and the other location in Travelers Rest offers Saturday yoga paired with mimosas. After a visit, you'll want The Community Tap to be your neighborhood watering hole.

The Community Tap - North Main
217 Wade Hampton Blvd., 864-631-2525

The Community Tap - Trailside at The Commons
147 Welborn St., 864-236-1375

The Community Tap - Travelers Rest
321-B S Main St., Travelers Rest, 864-689-1182

thecommunitytap.com

2

MAKE COCKTAIL HOUR A TWOFER

AT SWORDFISH COCKTAIL CLUB AND THE RABBIT HOLE

A duo of beautiful cocktail bars anchors two distinct Greenville neighborhoods. Swordfish Cocktail Club is on Coffee Street downtown, just a bit off Main Street. The nondescript low brick exterior belies an elegant cocktail club with aptly made drinks, extensive spirits, and pretty apps. They also produce their own super-sparkly seltzer water utilizing Greenville's "Cleanest Water in America." Go for a spirit-forward, stirred cocktail at Swordfish and take note of the perfectly selected glassware for each drink. The Rabbit Hole is an Alice in Wonderland–themed cocktail bar in West Greenville, which is part of a historic textile village. It's home to an over-the-top powder room worthy of a bathroom selfie and a wonderful boozy brunch. Go for a fruited cocktail. The drinks tend to be as pretty as the interiors. Sitting around the fire ring on the covered front patio is always fun, but don't forget to ask to walk down the clock-laden hallway to see the secret speakeasy in the back.

Swordfish Cocktail Club
220 E Coffee St., 864-434-9519, swordfishcocktails.com

The Rabbit Hole
1268 Pendleton St., 864-214-1797, therabbitholegvl.com

3

WATCH THE DOCUMENTARY *GREAT WALL* AND THEN DINE AT SUM BAR

Undercurrent Film Co. pulled off a hat trick when it won the James Beard Media Award for Documentary Short with its 16-minute film *Great Wall* about owner and chef Khailing Neoh opening a dim sum restaurant in downtown Greenville. The film and the food at Sum Bar are beautifully made, and seasonal dumplings really shine on the plate. A deconstructed crab rangoon is a winner, and the blistered green beans are tossed in an addictive spicy sweet brown sauce. Sesame balls and egg custard tarts are staples, but look for featured desserts and cocktails served in playful glassware and ceramics. During the day, Sum Bar morphs into a coffee bar called Coffee Coffee. Its offerings are international leaning, sourced from organic farmers, with Asian breakfast options and baked goods. January is a special time to visit Sum Bar. Chinese New Year is celebrated all month long with food and drink specials, as well as holiday decor, and culminates with a giant Lunar New Year celebration in the courtyard.

307 E Washington St., 864-860-1004
eatsumbar.com

HAPPY HOUR IT UP

AT CORAL

The West End is a part of downtown that sits south of the Reedy River. It's a bustling district best known for Fluor Field, home of the Greenville Drive, a Red Sox farm team with its own mini version of Boston's Fenway Park complete with the Green Monster wall. Happy hour is an institution in the West End, especially when The Drive has a home game. Coral has a lively happy hour with a crushable bar menu. Sliders, oysters, and crudo specials are produced by the same kitchen as its high-end dining room. Look for martini specials and opt to sit near the open windows at the sidewalk for primo people watching. The bread service here is notable with ocean butter and a crushable burger for less than $20. Seats turn over pretty quickly, so if stools aren't available, grab a drink and stand around a bit. Greenville locals are a friendly group, and you'll soon be chatting it up with several.

654 S Main St., 864-619-0017
coralgreenville.com

5

ORDER A POMEGRANATE MARTINI

AT POMEGRANATE ON MAIN

The beautiful Persian restaurant is a gem at lunch or dinner, especially with a group, but don't discount popping in for a signature Pomegranate Martini, made with vodka, pomegranate liquor, and pomegranate juice, and kept cold from the first sip to the last with a single frozen grape. There are lots of shareable apps to order here if you want to snack with drinks, including a trio of dips served with pita bread and fresh herbs. Ask your server to describe the options, which include mast khiyar, mirza ghasemi, borani spinach, kashk bademjan, and more. If you stay for dinner, consider the perfectly seared kabobs over rice. The outdoor patio features a tiled fountain and is a great place to hang out before or after a stroll through Falls Park. Reservations are recommended, especially during warm weather months if you want to sit on the patio.

618 S Main St., 864-241-3012
pomegranateonmain.com

OTHER GREAT PLACES TO DRINK

Wine House
475 Haywood Rd., Ste. 8, 864-451-7307
winehousegvl.com

Greenville Beer Exchange
7 S Laurens St., Ste. A, 864-232-3533
facebook.com/GBXbeer

Foxcroft Wine Co.
631 S Main St., 864-906-4200
foxcroftwine.com/greenville

The Whale - A Craft Beer Collective
1108 S Main St., Ste. 116, 864-263-7529
thewhalecollective.com

Liability Brewing Co.
109 W Stone Ave., Ste. D, 864-920-1599
liabilitybrewing.co

Carolina Bauernhaus
556 Perry Ave., 864-263-3389
carolinabauernhaus.com

Six & Twenty Distillery
556 Perry Ave., B103, 864-236-7886
sixandtwentydistillery.com

Other Lands
731 Rutherford Rd., 864-203-3642
otherlandsbrew.com

New Realm Brewing Company
912 S Main St., 803-258-6019
newrealmbrewing.com

6

WATCH A PANORAMIC SUNSET
AT JUNIPER

The bar at the top of the AC Hotel is visually stunning, and the opportunity to watch the sunset inside or out makes a stop here over the top. The decor is reset seasonally with inventive themes, but there are always nooks for two people or spaces for a dozen. The bar is aptly named for its nonstop bottles of, you guessed it, gin. This is a nice spot for apps, or stay for dinner. It is also a top spot for brunch and is featured on EATER Carolinas Greenville Brunch list. Cocktails are embellished with inventive garnishes like spun sugar wheels and interesting rims. Juniper is comfortable in the winter with fire tables and heaters, and easy in the summer with covered spaces and air-conditioning. Look for live performers of all ilk on weekend nights. Check the dress code for nighttime access before popping in. Juniper is, for sure, a seen-and-be-seen crowd.

315 S Main St., 864-549-0000
junipergvl.com

TIP

Line up for rooftop access outside of the AC Hotel just past the front doors. An elevator takes you directly to Juniper.

OTHER GREAT ROOFTOPS

SIP Whiskey & Wine
103 N Main St., Unit 400, 864-552-1916
sipgvl.com

UP on the Roof
250 Riverplace, 864-242-4000
eatupdrinkup.net

Hoppin' Greenville
120 N Markley St., Ste. 202, 864-243-8654
hoppingvl.com

W XYZ Bar at Aloft
5 N Laurens St., 864-315-2152
aloft-hotels.marriott.com

Eden Rooftop Lounge
21 E Coffee St., 864-438-4698
greenville.inknivy.com

Sweet Sippin'
103 W Curtis St., Simpsonville, 603-866-6785
facebook.com/sweetsippinsc

7

ENJOY CELEBRATED BREWS AT FIREFORGE CRAFTED BEER

Fireforge is a stellar small-batch beer bar with a sheltered patio that's worth spending an entire afternoon on. The former warehouse is right downtown, just off Main Street, replete with handmade tables indoors and out, and a pet-friendly biergarten. The kitchen, under the hand of chef Alex Morgan, offers a super menu to pair with craft beer, cider, mead, and seltzers. There are also specialty nonalcoholic options. Fireforge is known for their house-smoked Carolina trout dip, Reubens, and plays on fantastic grilled cheese sandwiches. They host lots of fun seasonal events like Oktoberfest and parties for Mardi Gras and Gasparilla, but there's always live music including jazz, bluegrass, and jam bands. But let's talk about the award-winning beer! Fireforge won two gold medals at the 2025 World Beer Championships, so if you want to taste these champs, look for the Baltic Porter and the seasonal flavored ale.

311 E Washington St., 864-300-4809
fireforge.beer

8

EAT A SHRIMP TACO
AT THE DROP-IN STORE

The unassuming convenience store just behind Horizon Records is a neighborhood hangout. During the week, Maria Gomes makes lunch in the back kitchen, and booths and tables fill up Monday through Friday. Though there are often Goan plates, like pumpkin curry and feijoada, green chili chicken enchiladas, and cheeseburgers, the reason to eat lunch at Maria's Kitchen at the Drop-In Store is for the spicy shrimp tacos. Lots of regulars drive in from all over for shrimp tacos, and you'll always bump into neighbors from the North Main area. In the evening, it's a place to meet up with friends for beer or to buy a bottle of wine. What's for sure is that you're never a stranger at the Drop-In Store once you've met Maria. Her son Anthony is fun to talk craft beer and wine with too; he's a serious traveler with deep knowledge.

709 N Main St., 864-242-011
facebook.com/thedropinstore

9

BRUNCH
AT FORK AND PLOUGH

Weekend brunch is an institution in Greenville, and Fork and Plough may be the very best of the bunch. It is a beloved neighborhood restaurant in Historic Overbrook with chef-owner Shawn Kelly at the helm. He is supplied by farmer and co-owner Roddy Pick of Kingbird Pastures. You'll eat like a local at every visit. There's eggs Benedict constructed over fluffy cathead biscuits, and a cheeseburger with mushrooms and arugula that's noteworthy. And don't skip on the beautiful cinnamon rolls and house-made pop tarts. To top it all off, Fork and Plough mimosas are delightful: Sparkling wine is poured over a square rocks orange juice ice cube. When you're ready for a refill, they'll happily top you off with more bubbles. Take note of the local art, all curated by Pick, which rotates each month. One hundred percent of sales go back to the artist. There's even art in the bathrooms.

1629 E North St., 864-609-4249
forkandplough.com

TIP

I like to sit at the bar, even with friends, but they do take reservations for both the dining room and the covered patio.

OTHER GREAT PLACES TO BRUNCH

The Bohemian Cafe
2B W Stone Ave., 864-233-0006
thebohemiancafe.com

Mr. Crisp
1501 E North St., Ste. 102, 864-549-8149
therealmrcrisp.com

Indaco
40 W Broad St., 864-326-4817
indacorestaurant.com

Soby's
207 S Main St., 864-232-7007
sobys.com

Nose Dive
116 S Main St., 864-373-7300
thenosedive.com

Larkin's
32 E Broad St., 864-467-9777
larkinsgvl.com

Stella's Southern Brasserie
340 Rocky Slope Rd., Ste. 100, 864-626-6900
stellasbrasserie.com

10

INDULGE
AT LARUE FINE CHOCOLATE

Tucked behind Pendleton Street in West Greenville is a bespoke chocolate shop that feels like much more than just a confectionery. Yes, there are oodles of handmade chocolates and truffles but there are also craft cocktails to pair with chocolate and cheeseboards and curated wine selections and other desserts. Opened by chocolatier Elizabeth Logan McDaniel, LaRue Fine Chocolate uses excellent ingredients, including local and organic products like Bee Well honey and Bulls Bay sea salt. Elizabeth's background as a Certified Specialist of Wine and her talent for unique flavor combinations really shows in every bite. The cozy café is an intimate environment, and it's just perfect for a good catch-up with a friend or a date, afternoon or evening. In addition to their Perry Avenue location, LaRue has expanded to The Commons near Unity Park. This location also offers ice cream and cookies.

LaRue Fine Chocolate
556 Perry Ave., Ste. B115, 864-263-7083

LaRue at The Commons
147 Welborn St.

laruefinechocolate.com

OTHER GREAT PLACES FOR SWEET TREATS

Spill the Beans
531 S Main St., 864-242-6355
stbdowntown.com

Clare's Creamery
1635 E North St.
clarescreamery.com

Old Europe Coffee & Desserts
716-A S Main St., 864-775-0210
oldeuropedesserts.com

The Chocolate Shoppe
1392 N Pleasantburg Dr., 864-292-0789
makingtheworldsweeter.com

Le Petit Croissant
640 S Main St., 864-520-1555
lepetitcroissantgreenville.com

Scout's Doughnuts
1700 E North St., 864-552-1021
scoutsdoughnuts.com

Strossner's
21 Roper Mountain Rd., 864-233-3996
strossners.com

Wildflower Cupcake and Dessert Bar
3730 Pelham Rd., 864-539-3458
greenvillecupcakes.com

11

DRINK THE CHEAPEST WINE IN GREENVILLE
AT NORTHHAMPTON WINE + DINE

The wineshop and restaurant tucked behind the underpass downtown on Broad Street has been selecting beautiful bottles for locals for decades. The expertise of the staff may be unsurpassed in Greenville, but the best reason to go to Northampton is for a $10 corkage fee over retail. Where most restaurants charge two and a half times retail for their bottle list and three to four times retail for a pour, Northampton expects its guests to stay and enjoy good wine at a really great price. The restaurant is known for a seafood chili app that you'll want to order two at a time and a white chocolate croissant bread pudding that's worth every calorie. Wine tastings often sell out, and oenophiles are seen here studying to become sommeliers.

211-A E Broad St., 864-271-3919
northamptonwineanddine.com

INHALE TACOS
AT COMAL 864

Chef Dayna Lee-Márquez moved to Greenville from the Rio Grande Valley. Her Brownsville, Texas, menu struck a chord with diners, and today she has two locations of Comal 864, one in the Water Tower District in an original textile mill general store and one in Midtown just a hop, skip, and a jump away from Radio Room, a popular music venue. "Comal" is a traditional Mexican griddle, and the chef takes full advantage of hers to create delicious seared meats and exquisite queso-birria tacos. There's birria ramen too and birria grilled cheese on telera bread. Breakfast tacos and breakfast burritos pull a crowd in the mornings, and a bar at the Midtown location, called Escorpion, produces an excellent cocktail program by barman Graham Stockley. Chef Dayna was nominated for Best Chef Southeast by the James Beard Foundation in 2023, in part for her community activism and passion for feeding local neighborhoods. Comal 864 was also named one of USA TODAY's 2025 Restaurant of the Year.

Comal 864 Woodside
1112 Woodside Ave., 864-214-1862

Comal 864 Midtown
219 W Antrim Dr., 864-236-7586

comal864.com

GET CRABBY
AT SOBY'S

The icon of downtown dining is Soby's New South Cuisine. It opened when little else was on Main Street, and for more than 25 years it has pleased locals and visitors alike with award-winning plates including an addictively good wet variety of crab cake. Its set includes haricot verts and maque choux, aka green beans and cream corn, and you will long think about it once you have left. Cheddar garlic biscuits and white chocolate banana cream pie take dinner here over the top. The building is notable too; it was a cotton warehouse that supported the textile industry along the Reedy River, and its original brick walls line the dining room. Brunch is super special at Soby's too. With the purchase of a full bottle of champagne, a fried chicken supper arrives to accompany it. Lastly, don't forget to peruse the Soby's 25th anniversary cookbook; it's a winner.

207 S Main St., 864-232-7007
sobys.com

14

SIT AT THE CHEF'S COUNTER
AT CAMP

Executive chef Diego Abel Campos is a celebrated chef, and his personality and cuisine really shine when you reserve a seat at the chef's counter at CAMP in Camperdown Plaza downtown. He was raised in Puebla, Mexico, and moved to Greenville when he was 11. The menu at CAMP is a romp of global flavors utilizing local ingredients, and the large restaurant hums along under his leadership. The small plates menu is shareable and features items like short ribs with fingerling potato, pork belly with gochujang, and tofu lettuce cups with chili crisp. A marinated olives and nuts snack is always a winner, and cocktails are creative and seasonally driven. It's a fun date to watch the action as these plates come together, and often the chef and his team will slip you several extra bites to try. Venture upstairs to a rooftop bar after dinner and watch the twinkle of the plaza below.

2 E Broad St., 864-514-2267
table301.com/camp

15

WATCH MAIN STREET FROM ABOVE

AT JIANNA

Chef Michael Kramer and GM Andrea Ciavardini-Royko are a splendid team at the lovely modern Italian restaurant Jianna. It is home to Greenville's prettiest balcony, which overlooks both Main Street and the entrance to Falls Park. Reserve a table for two outside and soak in Greenville's near perfect four seasons of weather. Featured entrées are not to be missed, and the entire wine list is Italian, by the glass or by the bottle. The bar is a fun, busy place to sit. One end includes an oyster bar that is top notch, and the restaurant never smells like seafood; it's a real magic trick. Pasta is extruded in-house and is cooked perfectly. A warm ricotta appetizer is a bestseller and has never come off the menu. Though the restaurant is on the second floor, if you don't want to traverse the stairs simply call the restaurant and they'll direct you to the elevator entrance.

600 S Main St., Floor 2, 864-720-2200
jiannagreenville.com

TIP
Nab a great souvenir; Jianna just published a full-color cookbook, and it is a love letter to cooking a restaurant-level dinner at home.

16

SLURP OYSTERS
AT THE JONES OYSTER CO.

Step inside Jones Oyster and feel immediately welcome. The nautical vibe is spot-on without being kitschy, and sitting at the bar is as comfortable as dining at a table. This is by far Greenville's best lunch spot, and you'll see it chock-full of locals, politicos, business types, dates, and group outings. The board shares what oysters are being shucked and served each day, but don't miss out on a menu full of delicious choices including two variations of lobster rolls, which utilize two types of mayonnaise: Duke's for the southern derivation and Hellman's for the northern. There're fantastic fried hush puppies full of corn. There's crab rice too and New Orleans–style grilled oysters. A wonderful by-the-glass wine list makes a sip here with a meal feel special, but what you won't get at Jones is a reservation, so plan to arrive early or hang out a bit on Court Street and wait.

22 E Court St., 864-549-0301
thejonesoysterco.com

17

DEVOUR A CATHEAD BISCUIT

AT MAVERICK

A cathead biscuit is square and extra big and extra fluffy. This occurs from utilizing cake flour to create loft, not sweetness. The ones at Maverick Biscuit are made from scratch each day and are tremendously good. Though there are two other locations, the original location in Taylors is my favorite. The biscuit shrimp and grits is delicious with the right amount of cream, heralding from a lobster sherry sauce, and a bit of heat. Biscuit sandwiches feature Tillamook cheddar, eggs, and a choice of fried chicken, breakfast meat, or fried bologna. There are biscuits and gravy too, with a choice of sawmill or sausage gravy; both are top notch. And don't forget about a fried green tomato biscuit with pimento cheese. The counter service restaurant is cheery and makes quick work of orders. When the weather is nice, it is great to sit outside on the front patio.

2818 Wade Hampton Blvd., Taylors, 864-631-1199
maverickbiscuit.com

18

ORDER IT ALL
AT SCOUNDREL

Chef Joe Cash returned to Greenville in 2022 after a star-studded culinary career in New York City working at Per Se and running kitchens for Major Food Group; he was executive chef at The Pool when the pandemic shuttered much of the city. He returned home with his young family to open Scoundrel, and it was quickly nominated for Best New Restaurant US by the James Beard Foundation. Interiors echo a modern French brasserie with mirrored surfaces and rounded edges. A lounge area is nice for a group and the bar offers a standout happy hour. There's a covered patio too, and private dining is available. Plates from starters to desserts are dressed to impress. Oysters are adroitly presented, as well as deviled crab, and the most perfect Caesar arrives with a snowy mountain of parmesan. There's steak au poivre and duck with lacinato kale and a cocoa powder cake that Cash says will never come off the menu (it's his grandmother's recipe).

18 N Main St., 864-283-0095
scoundrelgvl.com

TIP

Reservations are highly recommended, especially on Thursday, Friday, and Saturday.

OTHER GREAT PLACES TO GO ON A DATE

The Lazy Goat
170 Riverplace, 864-679-5299
thelazygoat.com

Between the Trees
44 E Camperdown Way, 864-603-1630
betweenthetrees.com

Maestro Bistro & Dinner Club
104 S Main St., Ste. 105, 864-248-0702
maestrobistroanddinnerclub.co

Sushi Go
247 N Main St., 864-631-1145
sushigousa.com

The 07
1010 Laurens Rd., 864-203-2491, the07gvl.com

Sirin Thai
1540 Wade Hampton Blvd., Ste. C, 864-631-1892
facebook.com/sirinthaigreenville

Patterson Kitchen + Bar
110 Halton Ave., 864-509-6484
facebook.com/pattersonhartness

Tavola Italian
620 Bridgeway Blvd., Simpsonville, 864-319-4648
tavolaitalian.com

Sushi-Masa Japanese Restaurant
8590 Pelham Rd., 864-288-2227
sushi-masa-japanese-restaurant.localid.top

White Wine & Butter
2299 E Gap Creek Rd., Greer, 864-417-4106
whitewineandbutter.com

19

GET OFF THE TRAIL
AT THE COMMONS

This is a food hall where you can get it all, any time of day. Early morning trail runners can stop in for Methodical coffee and breakfast or order a juice or smoothie at Kuka Juice. Stop in at midday for tacos at Automatic Taco or a slew of chef-driven burger and fries at GB&D. In the evening, there's beer and wine at Tapside Trail by The Community Tap. For dinner options, consider barbecue from MooHogz Craft BBQ or Indian street food at Indigo Kitchen. There are tapas at Paseo and pizza by Leo's. There's also ice cream from LaRue's second location at The Commons. They offer 10 house-made flavors as well as cookies and cookie ice cream sandwiches. The Commons is a great, well-lit place to park and hop right onto the Swamp Rabbit Trail, Greenville's urban rail trail. There's a playground and green space too; inside, community seating creates a fun vibe.

147 Welborn St., 864-203-5704
commonsgvl.com

TRY AFGHAN CUISINE
AT ARYANA

Feel transported to the rich culinary landscape of Afghanistan at Aryana on East Coffee Street in the heart of downtown Greenville. Chef and owner Nelo Mayar cooks Afghan street food with an eye for making recipes healthier. Everything at Aryana is made from scratch, and Mayar is a wizard at creating savory and layered sauces for each dish. There are delicate dumplings filled with meat and onion called mantu, topped with sweet peas, carrots, and house-made yogurt. There's a variety of kabobs served with the longest grain rice you've ever seen. Vegetarians and vegans feel well fed at Aryana. Each vegetable dish is sauced and plated as an entrée and served with rice, bread, and salad. The burani is stupendous, and the daal is some of the best I've ever eaten. There are desserts too, but don't skip on the cardamom iced tea. It's also available to buy by the half gallon.

210 E Coffee St., 864-236-7410
aryanagreenville.com

TIP

Chef Nelo published her own cookbook, so pick one up while you're at the restaurant. She is a natural storyteller.

21

BOOK A TABLE FOR SUNDAY DINNER

AT TOPSOIL

Its building was once Travelers Rest's original general store, Williams Hardware. Today, there's an open-concept kitchen and dining room with fantastic seating and beautiful interiors. Executive chef Adam Cooke was a 2020 James Beard semifinalist for Best Chef Southeast. His farm-to-table approach shines on the plate, and much on the menu is harvested from their very own farm, grown on 16 acres by owner Wendy Lynam. Topsoil is a lovely place to have brunch, and they host bluegrass brunch every Sunday, but getting a reservation for the dinner on a Sunday is where it is at! The Chef's Tasting Experience has been called a "culinary trust fall," and I would recommend adding the additional wine pairings curated by their excellent sommelier Lisa Simons. It's typically five courses that build upon what's in season. Also look for monthly Plant Based Dinners and other special events.

13 S Main St., Travelers Rest, 864-400-5424
topsoilrestaurant.com

DEVOUR CREPES
AT TANDEM

Tandem Crêperie & Coffeehouse is a beloved local spot in Travelers Rest known for its fantastic service, made-to-order crepes, and Counter Culture Coffee. The yellow coffee cups are iconic here, so make sure to take a photo holding one. Seating is often community-style, and you'll have fun chatting it up with locals, many who stopped off from riding the Swamp Rabbit Trail. There are sweet and savory crepes. Of course, the Nutella option is a big hit as is the lemon sugar crepe, but there are hearty breakfast crepes too filled with bacon, eggs, and cheese or one with rosemary and roasted root vegetables. There are plenty of hot and cold drink options available as well as whole-grain waffles and more bakery items. Parking can be crowded so consider parking on Main Street if you see a spot. The building was originally built as a post office in the 1940s.

2 Main St., Travelers Rest, 864-610-2245
tandemcc.com

GET SOME 'QUE
AT MIKE & JEFFS

Mike & Jeffs has been a barbecue institution in Greenville since 1996. It is in a neighborhood that some would call San Souci and others might call the Water Tower District. Meats are cooked over open hickory wood for 16 to 18 hours. There's pulled pork, smoked chicken, and varieties of ribs, as well as barbecue dogs and other specials. Sides include beans, slaw, mac and cheese, sweet potato casserole, and more. It is well known that you can drive by Mike & Jeffs and smell the woodsmoke and the barbecue cooking. The atmosphere is casual and friendly. A lot of customers arrive for takeout but stop in to say hi for a while. The restaurant is closed on Sundays and Mondays, which is typical for Greenville. Mike & Jeffs is on the SC BBQ Trail along with nearly 50 other historic places to eat barbecue.

2401 Old Buncombe Rd., 864-271-5225
mikeandjeffsbbq.com

OTHER GREAT PLACES TO GET 'QUE

Henry's Smokehouse
240 Wade Hampton Blvd., 864-232-7774
henryssmokehouse.com

Bucky's Bar-B-Q
1700 Roper Mountain Rd., 864-329-0054
buckysbbq.com

Home Team BBQ
815 Laurens Rd., 864-686-7427
hometeambbq.com

Lewis Barbeque
214 Rutherford St., 864-513-6045
lewisbarbeque.com

Smoky Dreams Barbeque
2131 Woodruff Rd., Ste. A, 864-627-4227
smokydreamsbbq.com

ORDER FRIED CHICKEN
AT OJ'S DINER

Known for mouthwatering comfort food and friendly, efficient service, OJ's Diner in West Greenville is only open Monday through Friday for lunch and dinner. Folks start lining up at lunch for OJ's fried chicken to drop right at 11 a.m. because once it's sold out, it's gone for the day. Delicious sides include mac and cheese, the most perfectly cooked cabbage, fried okra, and so much more. You'll be asked if you want a roll or corn bread, and the only acceptable answer is both. There are ribs and fried fish on Fridays. Cobbler changes seasonally. If you visit in the fall, ordering the sweet potato cobbler is a good call. Yes, there's a drive-through at OJ's Diner, but the dining room is where it's at. Go through the lunch line, pay at the end, and take a seat. You will be well taken care of with table service and unlimited tea refills.

907 Pendleton St., 864-235-2539
ojsdiner.com

TIP

OJ's has never left EATER's Essential 18 Restaurants for Greenville, SC, though nearly every restaurant has rotated off the list at some point!

DON'T UNWRAP THIS BAGEL
AT SULLY'S STEAMERS

The original location of Sully's Steamers is a gem, just behind Main Street. Their bagel sandwiches are sliced, built, wrapped, and then steamed in magical steamy machines until they are a delicious oozy mess. Slowly peel one open and eat it a bite at a time. There are lots of creative options from breakfast bagel sandwiches with eggs, cheese, and breakfast meats to lunch options with deli meat, spreads, and toppings. The Nacho Maximus is a local favorite stuffed with turkey, cheddar, lettuce, honey mustard, parm-peppercorn dressing, and a half bag of nacho cheese Doritos. There are combinations for vegetarians too, and things that kids are drawn to like pizza bagels and PB&J. Sully's is a fun place to hang out in the heart of Greenville and stays open late, on Fridays and Saturdays until 3 a.m. Make sure to check out their statement of beliefs cleverly posted as the "Ultimate Steamer." It's one-part good food, combined with nice people, community, a servant's heart, and lots of napkins.

6 E Washington St., 864-509-6061
sullyssteamers.com

PAIR A COFFEE AND BEER

AT GRATEFUL BREW

The Midmod building sits across the street from Greenville Technical College on Pleasantburg Drive and is an adorable stop for coffee in the morning that transitions over to beer and drinks as the day goes on. It's a coffee shop and taproom all in one, and its sloped entrance is a distinctive feature. There are delicious coffee drinks, tea, and more, including pastries and house-made syrups. This is a great place to jump on the WiFi and work for a while. You can for sure feel the sense of community here. At night, there's craft beer, cider, wine, and nonalcoholic canned drinks. Check the calendar for food trucks out front; the patio is a fun place to eat. Locals know Grateful Brew as the spot next to Pita House, a beloved Mediterranean restaurant that is family owned and operated. The chopped salad, grape leaves, and gyro pita sandwiches hit the spot.

501 S Pleasantburg Dr., 864-558-0767
gratefulbrewgvl.com

CARB LOAD
AT RISE BAKERY

West Greenville is becoming known for its independent dining scene, and Rise Bakery is one of the most notable restaurants. Its composed and delicious pastry—and significant bread program—have really garnered the attention of a loyal following. It all started as a pandemic passion project of owner Julian Loué; he turned a home baking hobby into a thriving business. The artisan and naturally leavened breads are baked each morning, and his staff begins arriving at 3:45 a.m. Croissants, cookies, and pastries are displayed in the front case; a twisted cardamom bun is a local favorite. There's a chocolate chip sourdough cookie too and a delicious morning bun. More than two dozen restaurants utilize Rise's sourdough bread on their menus, all baked and delivered by the dedicated staff. The kitchen is open to the storefront, and it's fun to order an espresso and watch the action.

1264 Pendleton St., 864-631-1690
risebakerysc.com

28

LUNCH WITH A CAUSE
AT JASMINE KITCHEN

The social enterprise café is also a sunny and adorable place to lunch. Jasmine Kitchen offers job training and employment to women who have endured human trafficking or addiction. Jasmine Road is its parent organization, best known for a two-year residential program for survivors. Many participants go on to train and ultimately work full-time in the restaurant. The historic cottage is a century-old building renovated into a modern restaurant. The dining room is replete with a mural painted by local artist Jean Wilson Freeman, who is well known for her whimsical florals. Order the café's combo plate and watch it arrive with a half sandwich, soup, salad, and a generous wedge of pound cake. It's a winner. Soup offerings change every week, and don't forget to stop by the retail alcove for meaningful handmade gifts.

503 Augusta St., 864-263-3374
jasminekitchen.org

TIP

Jasmine Kitchen also has its own parking lot, so it's an easy place to meet up for lunch in the downtown area.

OTHER GREAT PLACES FOR LUNCH

Asada
903 Wade Hampton Blvd., 864-770-3450
asadarestaurant.com

Kitchen Sync
1609 Laurens Rd., 864-568-8115
kitchensyncgreenville.com

Trio – A Brick Oven Cafe
22 N Main St., 864-467-1000
triocafe.com

Society Sandwich Bar & Social Club
18 E Coffee St., 864-203-7046
societygvl.com

Windy City Burgers
12 E Coffee St., 864-349-1390
windycityburgers.com

Birrieria 101
2301 Wade Hampton Blvd., 864-991-8036
facebook.com/birrieria101

Zorba Lounge
1414 E Washington St., 864-233-3125

Pita House
495 S Pleasantburg Dr., 864-271-9895
pitahousesc.com

Sushi-Masa Japanese Restaurant
8590 Pelham Rd., 864-288-2227
sushi-masa-japanese-restaurant.localid.top

DOUBLE DOWN
AT HARRY'S HOAGIE SHOPPE AND MIKE'S CHEESESTEAKS

For a true taste of Philly right in Greenville, head to Harry's Hoagie Shoppe and Mike's Cheesesteaks in Historic Overbrook. It's a two-for-one concept at the shop on East North Street. Get here early or expect to wait in line at lunchtime. An emphasis on premium meats and cheeses from Italy keeps the crowd coming back again and again. Sesame rolls are sourced from New Jersey's Liscio's Bakery. There are classic Italian hoagies, stuffed with a variety of meats and dressed with oil, vinegar, and onions. There's potato salad too and pickled giardiniera. On the Mike's side, the Philly cheesesteaks are a standout. There are roast pork sandwiches too, which I really love. Both arrive ideally hot, and leftovers are rarely seen. But take note, the sandwich shop has limited hours on Sundays and is closed on Mondays.

1700 E North St., 864-907-1499
mikescheesesteaks.com

GO COFFEE TASTING
AT COFFEE UNDERGROUND AND METHODICAL

Two of Greenville's most celebrated coffee spots sit across the street from each other. Coffee Underground was opened by Dana Lowie way back in 1991, when Greenville was barely the whisper of the Main Street it is today. Still beloved for hand-produced espresso drinks, it's an underground mecca for locals to hang out, work, and snack. They also offer extraordinary desserts. Methodical is at the back of the One Plaza in a gorgeous, tiled space. Their coffee drinks arrive in blue-and-white china cups with a cloth napkin and a real spoon. The art of coffee is expressed here, so take time to enjoy the aroma and the experience. Methodical is an award-winning coffee roaster and known for calling on regional artists to design their package art, such as fine artist Annie Koelle. Can you do two coffee shop stops in a day? For sure, I'd recommend them back-to-back.

Coffee Underground
1 E Coffee St., 864-298-0494
coffeeunderground.info

Methodical
101 N Main St., Ste. D, 864-349-1913
methodicalcoffee.com

Radio Room Music
Credit Rob MacDonald

MUSIC AND ENTERTAINMENT

31

KICK-START YOUR WEEKEND
AT SATURDAY MARKET

The award-winning Saturday Market takes over blocks of Main Street from 8 a.m. to noon on Saturdays, three seasons a year, with more than 75 vendors. Farmers, growers, and makers sell produce and proteins, flowers, cheese, jam, coffee, and gifts, but locals show up to buy Naked Pasta ravioli from Chris and Brett Barest. The tiny pasta company makes hyperseasonal ravioli for the farmers market; look for flavors like smoked brisket, ricotta lavender, and vegan fajita sweet potato. Other notable vendors include Colonial Milling for grits, Gibson Organic Farms for beef, Banana Manna for 15 choices of banana bread, and Bioway Farm for beautiful produce. Check the calendar for cooking demonstrations, events, and live music. The market is stroller friendly, but it is not dog friendly, so please leave your pups behind. Saturday Market really is an experience that captures the spirit of Greenville and its commitment to buy local.

May through October
Main St. at McBee Ave.
saturdaymarketlive.com

BUY A TICKET
FOR EUPHORIA

Each September, Greenville transforms into a mecca of dining, drinking, and music when Euphoria, a food, beverage, and music festival, occurs. For the past 25 years, Euphoria has scheduled four days of fun, and most events sell out. But throughout the year, Euphoria hosts satellite events seasonally and continues to give grants to the community. It was the brainchild of restaurateur Carl Sobocinski and musician Edwin McCain and is a celebrated organization. There are a range of experiences from daytime tastings, classes, and casual events to multicourse sit-down dinners, concerts, performances, and more. Feast by the Field is one of the best and allows guests to try dishes from dozens of restaurants, both local and visiting. Notable chefs have cooked at Euphoria including James Beard winners, Michelin-starred chefs, and Food Network stars. Chef Tyler Florence, who grew up in Greenville, has headlined the event, as well as Emeril Lagasse, Thomas Keller, and Curtis Duffy.

euphoriagreenville.com

TIP

If you can't make it to Greenville in the fall, consider Euphoria's February event, called Southern Remedy, which showcases local culinary talent, with music and paired drinks.

GET UP CLOSE TO LOCAL ARTISTS
AT ART & LIGHT GALLERY

The West Greenville gallery, in its converted 1932 millhouse on Aiken Street, is home to the work of 50-plus living Southern artists. Founded by artist Teresa Roche and curated by gallerists Bracken Stansberry and Kat Mazonne, the women of Art & Light have been featured in multiple publications for their extraordinary spaces, shows, collaborations, and art consultation. Roche began her career as a dancer, and her multimedia works exhibit a movement of grace that's distinctive. The gallery is open to the public Tuesday through Saturday. Browse the rooms, workshops, studios, and grounds, which include an exterior mural by artist Sunny Mullarkey McGowan and Eva Magill-Oliver. Photos are encouraged, children are welcome to their rotating shows, and art is available for sale at every price point. Notable artists include Diane Condon Kilgore, Rachael Van Dyke, Glory Day Loflin, Katie Walker, and photographer Eli Warren. This is a great Instagram account to follow too.

16 Aiken St., 864-252-5858
artandlightgallery.com

CATCH A SHOW
AT RADIO ROOM

Since 2012, Radio Room has been a premier midsize venue in the Upstate for regional bands. Now in their third and much bigger location in Midtown, owners David Raghib, Geoff Cannada, and Wes Gilliam can accommodate up to 500 listeners. Known for an eclectic lineup of 15 to 20 shows a month, Radio Room is a great place to experience live music, with a group, a date, or even solo. So many locals hang out here that there's always someone interesting to chat with. Acts like Rainbow Kitten Surprise, Shovels and Rope, and the Mountain Goats have played here. I recently heard Hot 8 Brass Band, a renowned jazz band from New Orleans. There are tribute bands too, which are a load of fun. The stage is 24 feet across, and the 16-foot ceilings of this former furniture store offer great acoustics. But the greatest feature of all might be the easy and ample parking.

28 Liberty Ln., 864-768-3568
radioroomgreenville.com

SING LIVE BAND KARAOKE

AT SMILEYS ON THE ROXX

When Smileys lost their lease in the West End, Greenville thought it might lose the stellar small music venue. Thankfully another local business stepped in and offered Smileys a partnership. It was August 2023 when On the Roxx said, Hey, Smileys, come aboard, and the rest is history. Smileys on the Roxx is a fantastic place to drink, grab some casual fare, and hear great live music seven nights a week. While there is a variety of bands, two events weekly really stand out: open mic night on Mondays and live band karaoke on Wednesdays. This is not your average karaoke; the band can make even the mediocre sound great. Fabulous performers do show up to take down the house, but some convenient volume control and backup vocals help every performer along. There are lots of TVs to watch sports too and you'll always find an avid fan here. Notably, the kitchen stays open until 2 a.m.

734 S Main St., 864-351-0541
smileysroxx.com

TIP
In Greenville on a Tuesday? Go see Charles Hedgepath and Friends starting at 7:30 at Smileys on the Roxx.

36

HANG OUT
AT THE PEACE CENTER COMPLEX

The six-acre campus is at the very center of downtown. It's comprised of the main concert hall; a smaller stage called the Gunter Theatre, which seats about 400; and then an outdoor stage right on the Reedy River with tiered open seating for another 1,200. There are multiple other venues in the works, but even the plaza out front can be utilized for performance art. The Broadway Series comes through every year with fantastic musicals including family favorites like The Lion King and Hamilton, Wicked, and more. The concert hall holds around 2,000 across three levels and multiple boxes. The acoustics have been called state of the art. There are concerts, opera, dance, comedy, film, chamber music, and so much more. If you snag a reservation across the river on the patio at the Lazy Goat, you can experience dinner and a show. Great bands play on the outdoor stage each summer. Last year, we heard Dawes here.

300 S Main St., 864-467-3000
peacecenter.org

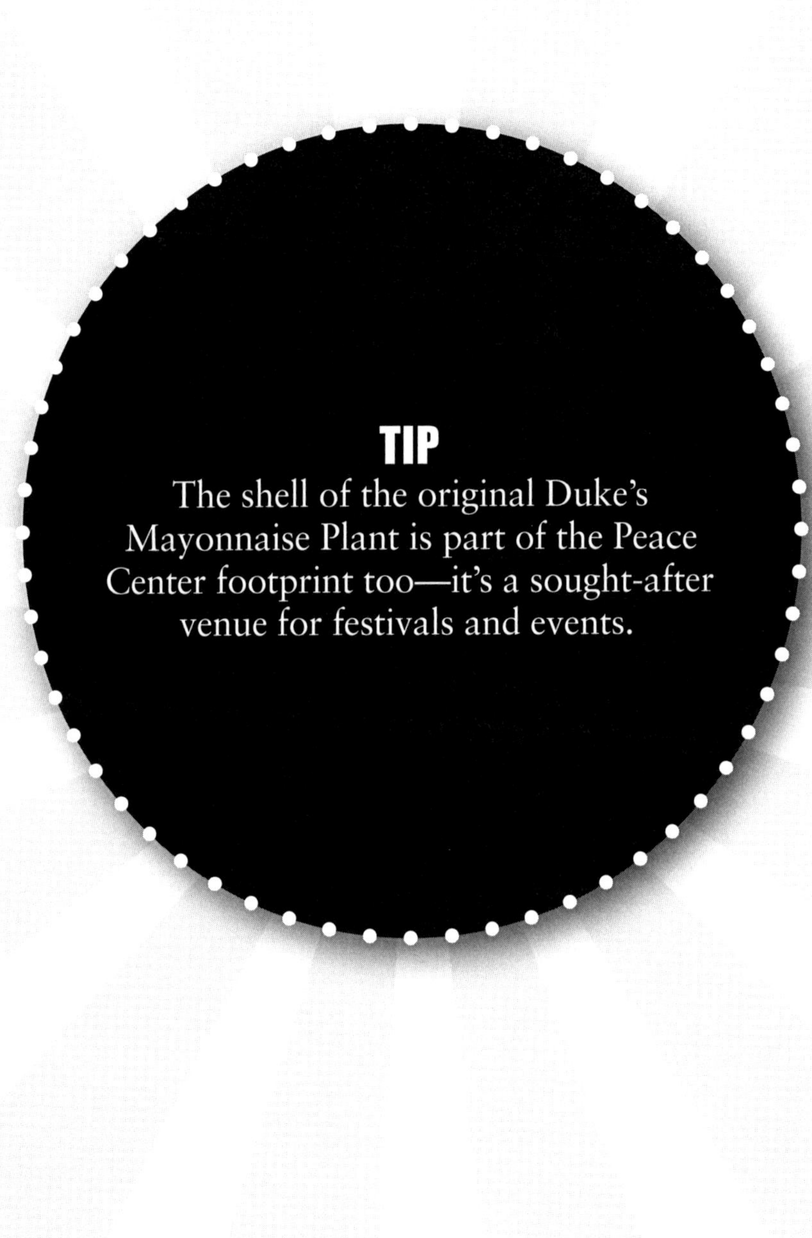

TIP

The shell of the original Duke's Mayonnaise Plant is part of the Peace Center footprint too—it's a sought-after venue for festivals and events.

SNAP A SELFIE
AT THE STONE MURAL PROJECT

Stone Avenue is lined with murals big and small because of a unique arts initiative by its magnet arts elementary school, Stone Academy. Started in 2014 with the help of PTA and the City of Greenville Art in Public Places Commission, graduating fifth graders assist working artists to paint vibrant murals on the side of commercial buildings. The result is some of the best backdrops in Greenville to snap a photo against. Notable murals include Joseph Bradley's goldfinches at the Westone development, Jean Wilson Freeman's otherworldly florals on the United Building, Sunny Mullarkey McGowan's monochrome life cycle of the butterfly at Hammock Law Firm, and Eric Benjamin's ode to Georges Seurat at the Prisma Pharmacy building. Other artists, like Michelle Jardines and Annie Koelle, jumped into the fun and painted more murals. More than 1,000 fifth graders have contributed to the public works of art, and the Stone Mural Project produced some of Greenville's very first murals.

The Stone Mural Project is included on the website for Art in Public Places Commission at greenvillesc.gov.

CATCH A SHOW
AT A LOCAL THEATER

There is a play for every taste in Greenville with year-round productions, and three of Greenville's best theaters offer calendars full of shows. Greenville Theatre is on the Heritage Green Campus along with the county museum, the children's museum, and the Hughes Main Library. Centre Stage feels more like a black box theater, and its lobby and venue spaces also act as a gallery for regional artists. The Warehouse Theatre is in West End. They publish a full season of plays each year and are known for original productions and a drama-heavy schedule. They also run the Upstate Shakespeare Festival in Falls Park every summer since 1998. Newer to town is the South Carolina New Play Festival, which has succeeded in bringing the future of American theater to the Upstate region. It is dedicated to giving an audience to new works across a multitude of stages in Greenville, including these three great playhouses.

Greenville Theatre
444 College St., 864-233-6238, greenvilletheatre.org

Centre Stage
501 River St., 864-233-6733, centrestage.org

The Warehouse Theatre
37 Augusta St., 864-235-6948, warehousetheatre.com

southcarolinanewplayfestival.org

39

EXPERIENCE
MAIN STREET FRIDAYS

Originally this event was called Friday Night Jazz, but as the City of Greenville added dates, they expanded the offerings and rebranded it Main Street Fridays at Noma Square. Today it happens in the plaza in front of the Hyatt Regency hotel and spills out onto Main Street, which is closed to traffic for two blocks. At one end there are inflatables for kids and at the other are beverage tents. Lots of folks bring their folding chairs and enjoy the music as the sun sets. It is a free event, and happy residents show up every Friday night from March until October. The weekly event runs from 5:30 p.m. until about 9:30 p.m. I like to go early and then head off to a dinner reservation downtown. Mac Arnold & Plate Full O' Blues is known to play as well as tribute bands like Jazzy Trinity, which plays Stevie Wonder tunes.

greenvillesc.gov

SING YOUR HEART OUT
AT THE WELL

I remember when this massive venue was built, and it was called the Bi-Lo Center. Today, it's the Bon Secours Wellness Arena or "The Well." It is home base for our minor-league hockey team, the Greenville Growl. It also hosts serious sporting events and major concerts. Greenville is lucky to be an easy stop between Atlanta and Charlotte, so The Well gets nearly every major musical act. I've seen Garth Brooks here and the Avett Brothers, my daughter saw Chris Stapleton at the arena, and friends enjoyed the Lumineers and Stevie Nicks. The SEC Women's Basketball tournament comes back again and again, and likely its proximity to downtown—it's just a few blocks off Main Street—makes it undeniably attractive to events. It can seat around 16,000 guests, and its economic impact exceeds $60 million.

650 N Academy St., 864-241-3800
bonsecoursarena.com

CAMP
AT THE ALBINO SKUNK FEST

This music festival, held twice a year, is known for booking up-and-coming bands, many of which have made it big time. Think Avett Brothers, Sam Bush, Watchhouse, and the Wood Brothers. Skunk Fest, as it's referred to locally, is cherished for offering a wide range of acts including folk, Americana, bluegrass, and Southern rock at its festivals in May and October. The vibe is laid back and family friendly. There are options to camp and stay the whole weekend too; even RVs are permitted. Local food vendors set up, and craft beer and other artisanal goods are sold throughout the weekend. The picturesque outdoor setting is postcard perfect. Pastoral splendor at its finest. It was founded in 1995 by Zig Zeigler as a private event but is now ticketed to the public. The funny name comes from Zeigler noticing mostly white skunks on the property.

4067 Jordan Rd., Greer, 864-895-5775
albinoskunk.com

GET YOUR BARD ON
AT SHAKESPEARE IN THE PARK

Officially the Upstate Shakespeare Festival by the Warehouse Theatre, three plays a year are staged in Falls Park along the Reedy River, just past the waterfalls. From May throughout the summer, performances happen on Thursday, Friday, and Saturday nights at 7 p.m. Bring blankets, chairs, and picnics; alcohol is allowed in clear cups with the purchase of a $1 wristband. Shakespeare in the Park, as locals refer to it, is more than 25 years old and a summer tradition in Greenville. With the belief that Shakespeare's themes are forever relevant, actors don contemporary clothing with minimal sets. Performances are free and run two hours. A mix of comedies and tragedies are scheduled each year and celebrated voraciously by area theatergoers.

warehousetheatre.com

Fluor Field
Credit Christen Clinkscales

SPORTS AND RECREATION

CATCH A BALL
AT FLUOR FIELD

Fluor Field is a mini Fenway Park, replete with a replica of the Green Monster wall in left field. The team moved into the downtown stadium in 2006, when it was named the Greenville Drive. It is a Boston Red Sox affiliate and plays in the South Atlantic League. The team has a passionate fan base, and a bunch of big leaguers have spent time with The Drive, such as Mookie Betts, Andrew Benintendi, and Rafael Devers. The team has clinched several division titles and won the league championship in 2017. But the other reason to go is to watch sunsets turn into fireworks. Across downtown you know when The Drive beats an opponent: The booms go off (though on Friday nights there is always a fireworks show). Lawn seating feels like a slice of Americana, and there's even a playground inside the stadium. Concessions all hail from local restaurants, and with the entrance of an $8 "Lawn and Deck" ticket, The Drive stadium is one of Greenville's best-attended happy hours.

945 S Main St., 864-240-4500
milb.com

44

VISIT THE HOME
OF SHOELESS JOE JACKSON

The life and career of baseball legend Shoeless Joe Jackson is celebrated at his home, which was relocated next to the Greenville Drive stadium in 2006. The modest brick house was originally located on East Wilburn Street, about three miles away. Shoeless Joe was born in South Carolina in 1887. As an outfielder with an incredible batting record, he maintained one of the highest batting averages in MLB history at .356. He is most widely associated with the 1919 Black Sox Scandal, though many in the area believe he didn't participate in throwing the World Series. The Shoeless Joe Jackson Museum and Baseball Library displays memorabilia, documents, and artifacts from his life, his childhood growing up in South Carolina, and his controversial ban from baseball. It is interestingly also a research center for baseball historians and houses more than 2,000 volumes dedicated to the game. You'll also learn how the player earned his famous moniker.

356 Field St., 864-288-6470
shoelessjoejackson.org

TIP

The home and museum are only open to the public on Saturdays from 10 a.m. to 2 p.m., but call ahead to schedule a private tour during the week.

CHIP AWAY
AT 3'S GREENVILLE GOLF AND GRILL

The fabulous and fun 12-hole, par 3 golf course on Villa Road experienced a full makeover in 2020 by renowned course architect Jeff Lawrence, with the help of an investment by Justin Timberlake and 8AM Golf. It was originally opened in 1997. The new design also includes a 16,500-square-foot putting course inspired by the one at St. Andrews as well as a 6.5-acre short game practice range. There are three types of natural turf maintained—Diamond Zoysia, bentgrass, and TifEagle Bermuda—for the extra nerdy golfer. And the course is illuminated for night games; lights stay on until 10:30 p.m. The Grubhouse offers a celebrated smash burger, as well as craft cocktails, a lobster grilled cheese on a griddled croissant, and an impressive selection of brown liquor for whiskey-drinking adults. It was famously featured on social media by Rebecca and Greg Remmey of @devourpower with their audience of more than two million followers.

61 Villa Rd., 864-233-6336
3s.golf

GET OUTSIDE
AT UNITY PARK

The newest park in Greenville is Unity Park. It offers a massive 60 acres of green space and expands the footprint of what feels like downtown. There are sports fields and playgrounds and walking trails and picnic areas, including a splash pad that operates from May through October. The Unity Bridge spans the Reedy River and connects the park on two sides. The Thomas and Vivian A. Wong Honor Tower is its newest feature. It is 10 stories high, and its observation deck offers stunning views of the Blue Ridge Mountains and downtown Greenville. It's meant to stand as a symbol of unity; its location was strategically placed at the midpoint of where Mayberry Park and Meadowbrook Park once stood, two parks that were historically segregated. The tower, designed by Endrestudio, accomplishes its twisting shape utilizing layers of wood screening; it's a workout of a climb! There is also a 10,000-square-foot welcome center often used as an event space.

320 S Hudson St., 864-232-2273
unityparkgreenville.com

47

HIKE

PARIS MOUNTAIN STATE PARK

About five miles north of downtown is Paris Mountain State Park. Its 1,500-plus acres of nature are something to experience all four seasons. The park is well maintained and offers walking and hiking trails, camping, lake swimming, biking, foraging, a music series, family programming, and more. It was established in 1935, and there are buildings to visit erected by the Civilian Conservation Corps (CCC) during the Great Depression. The 15 miles of trails come in all lengths and skill levels. The Sulphur Springs Loop offers scenic views, and the Brissy Ridge Loop is deeper in the park, harder to locate, and offers a bit less foot traffic on the trail. The park's 13-acre lake is partitioned for swimming and boating for canoes, kayaks, and pedal boats. A 40-site family campground is available for tent camping or RVs. At the top of the park sits Camp Buckhorn with its own lake; the picturesque group facility includes a historic lodge and 10 rustic cabins.

2401 State Park Rd., 864-244-5565
southcarolinaparks.com/paris-mountain

OTHER GREAT PLACES TO GO FOR A HIKE

Caesars Head State Park
8155 Geer Hwy., Cleveland, 864-836-6115
southcarolinaparks.com/caesars-head

Bald Rock Heritage Preserve
6600 Geer Hwy., Cleveland, 864-654-1671
visitgreenvillesc.com/listing/bald-rock-heritage-preserve/14246

Jones Gap State Park
303 Jones Gap Rd., Marietta, 864-836-6115
southcarolinaparks.com/jones-gap

Conestee Nature Preserve
840 Mauldin Rd., 864-277-2004
conesteepreserve.org

Cedar Falls Park Trail
201 Cedar Falls Rd., Fountain Inn, 864-288-6470
greenvillerec.com/parks/cedar-falls

HOP ON THE SWAMP RABBIT TRAIL

The 28-mile urban greenway follows the Reedy River and connects Greenville to Travelers Rest. It began in 2009 utilizing a defunct railroad corridor and provided walkers, runners, bikers, and stroller pushers a scenic way to get outside and away from vehicle traffic. Today it passes through Falls Park, Cleveland Park, and the campus of Furman University. It is sponsored by Prisma Health System and maintained by Greenville County Parks and Rec, which provides an interactive map of the trail online. Parts of the trail include installed rubber matting for a cushioned run; there are art and nature facts too. Linky Stone Park, also known locally as "the Children's Garden," is a good spot to enter the Swamp Rabbit Trail. When you need a break, stop at Swamp Rabbit Cafe & Grocery. It's a delicious café-coffee-pizza-bakery-and-more business, owned by two enterprising women, Mary Walsh and Jac Oliver. On the grocery side, find local goods from more than 300 farmers, ranchers, and makers.

Prisma Health Swamp Rabbit Trail
864-232-2273, greenvillerec.com/swamprabbit

Swamp Rabbit Cafe & Grocery
205 Cedar Lane Rd., 864-255-3385, swamprabbitcafe.com

49

MOUNTAIN BIKE GATEWAY PARK

This park in Travelers Rest is super fun for mountain bikers of all skill levels. Gateway Park offers a bike skill flow park within its boundaries, which they call a "progressive trail system." My kids loved it and got especially good at maneuvering the course. There's a figure-eight pump track, cross-country trails, and a skills development track, all with a mix of terrains. Everything here is sized for adults, but children who are comfortable on a bike will enjoy it too. There are other typical park amenities like playgrounds, picnic areas, sports fields. Gateway is also a good access point to get on the Swamp Rabbit Trail with its excellent parking. The park is located right behind Sunrift Adventures, which is a great outfitter store, and close to the original location of Sidewall Pizza, with a wonderful menu of artisan-made pizza, salads, and ice cream.

115 Henderson Dr., Travelers Rest, 864-288-6470
greenvillerec.com/parks/gateway-park

WIN A MATCH
AT PKL PARK

Adjacent to Greenville Unity Park is PKL Park, a well-planned and good-looking place to play pickleball, eat, drink, meet up with friends, and soak in some South Carolina sunshine at its open-air facility. Currently there are eight state-of-the-art, lighted courts. You can become a member or simply pay by the hour. There's instruction and a pro shop for all your pickleball needs. PKL Park offers not one but three dining options: the Kitchen at Mark V Studio, Toastified, and Coop's Crazy Chicken. The bar program includes adorably named cocktails like Pickle Me Sour. There's also a 100-square-foot lawn, live music events, and outdoor yard games like cornhole, table tennis, and giant Jenga. PKL Park overlooks Mayberry Field at Unity Park, and you really feel like part of the Unity Park neighborhood when you're here.

78 Mayberry St., 864-203-7149
pklparkgvl.com

51

TRAVERSE CLEVELAND PARK

Established in 1922 along the Reedy River, Cleveland Park is the city's largest municipal park. It spans from the zoo's entrance off East Washington Street all the way up to where it connects to Falls Park, which faces Main Street downtown. Its 122 acres is a mixed facility of exercise trails, natural woods, athletic fields, playgrounds, tennis and pickleball, basketball, planted gardens, sculpture, and more. Richland Creek also runs through the park. It was named after William Choice Cleveland, who donated nearly all of the crescent-shaped parcel. Highlights today include the Greenville Zoo, Rock Quarry Garden with its natural trickling waterfall, the Vietnam Veterans Memorial—and, of course, the Swamp Rabbit Trail winds through it all. The granite at the Rock Quarry Garden is believed to have been mined during the Civil War; it is a popular spot to get married in springtime and autumn months.

150 Cleveland Park Dr., 864-467-4355
greenvillesc.gov/1581/Cleveland-Park

HEAD TO HERDKLOTZ PARK

This park in northeast Greenville is especially fun for older kids, adults, and active families. First off, the soccer fields are pristine, and lots of leagues use them. There are sand volleyball courts too. The covered picnic seating can seat 75, and there are large, clean bathrooms and a half-mile walking loop around it all, but locals go to Herdklotz Park to play. The playgrounds are challenging, interactive, really big, and the slides barrel you down to the ground. Interestingly, it was once the site of Hopewell Sanitarium. You can still see ruins of the hospital's root cellar, and there is some signage posted to read up on it. The park was dedicated to Dick Herdklotz, a former county councilman and a champion of recreation facilities. The park boasts lovely views of both downtown Greenville and Paris Mountain and is especially pretty at sunset.

126 Beverly Rd., 864-288-6470
greenvillerec.com

53

EXPLORE A SECRET GARDEN

Abutting the Reedy River downtown is Linky Stone Park, or as locals call it, "the Children's Garden." Its 1.7 acres are located at 24 Reedy View Drive, and there's parking curbside. I share this because it is a bit hidden until you navigate to it at the intersection of West Broad and Richardson. It presents a storybook theme with sensory gardens like Hansel and Gretel's cottage, for example. There's also a geology wall to climb, made of area rocks and minerals and fossils. There are installed musical instruments to explore and stunning bronze statuary. Native plants are featured here as well as herbs, and visitors of all ages are encouraged to touch, pinch, and smell them. This is one of the best spots to enter the Swamp Rabbit Trail with kids.

24 Reedy View Dr., 864-232-2273
greenvillesc.gov

54

GO WILD
AT THE GREENVILLE ZOO

Across 14 acres, the Greenville Zoo is simply adorable. This is a zoo you can zip through in an hour or where you can spend an entire afternoon, and the ticket price is not prohibitive. There are diverse animals and scenery to take in, including 300 animals of 90 species including lions, red pandas, birds, reptiles, and monkeys of all kinds. It is committed to conservation and is involved in various international breeding programs including a giraffe exchange, which Greenville has embraced with naming contests and a live giraffe cam. The zoo first opened its gates in 1960 and lies within the footprint of Cleveland Park. The zoo also is part of some significant civil rights history. When Black residents pushed the city to integrate a municipal swimming pool at the park, it was instead scooped inside the zoo to create a sea lion exhibit, which no longer exists. Hopefully a historical marker can be added to commemorate its location.

150 Cleveland Park Dr., 864-467-4300
greenvillezoo.com

TIP

The parking is free at Greenville Zoo; isn't that incredible? There are also two very nice, accessible parks right out front and often an ice cream stand.

PICK A BOUQUET
AT SASSAFRASS FLOWER FARM

Sarah DuBose operates the most beautiful flower farm in nearby Easley. Its pastoral setting is picture perfect, and there's a covered shelter with a fireplace for events. Sarah cultivates seasonal flowers and, unlike many flower farms, sells to the public as well as wholesales to the trade. Sassafrass hosts U-pick events as well, and they are a hit. You get to clip your own flowers and learn to make bouquets. There are often food trucks and music, and sometimes yoga, wine tastings, or children's activities. Most U-picks occur May through October, but Sarah is always growing something like curly willow or making dried mixes and wreaths. You can reserve a private pick as well. Could anything be more romantic? The property is an ideal setting for picnics too. Sassafrass delivers farm-fresh bouquets to lots of local stores as well, such as Swamp Rabbit Grocery and the Cook's Station.

255 Alex Dr., Easley
sassafrassflowerfarm.com

FILL A BUCKET OF BERRIES
AT BEECHWOOD FARMS

This family farm in Marietta, just a bit north of Greenville, is known for its fresh produce and specifically for its strawberry fields. Lots of school groups head here, but you can go any day of the week but Sundays during berry season, typically starting in early May. A long-standing tradition prompts families to visit specifically on one Sunday: Mother's Day. This is when Beachwood Farms passes out bowls of free homemade strawberry shortcake to all visitors. Their fields are a great spot for a family photo too. The farm also grows fantastic corn, tomatoes, squash, and more and sells pickles and honey and other sundry items. They operate tables at several of the farmers markets, such as Greenville's Saturday Market, and allow their grandchildren and other teenage employees to keep the profits for college tuition.

204 Bates Bridge Rd., Marietta, 864-836-6075
mybeechwoodfarms.com

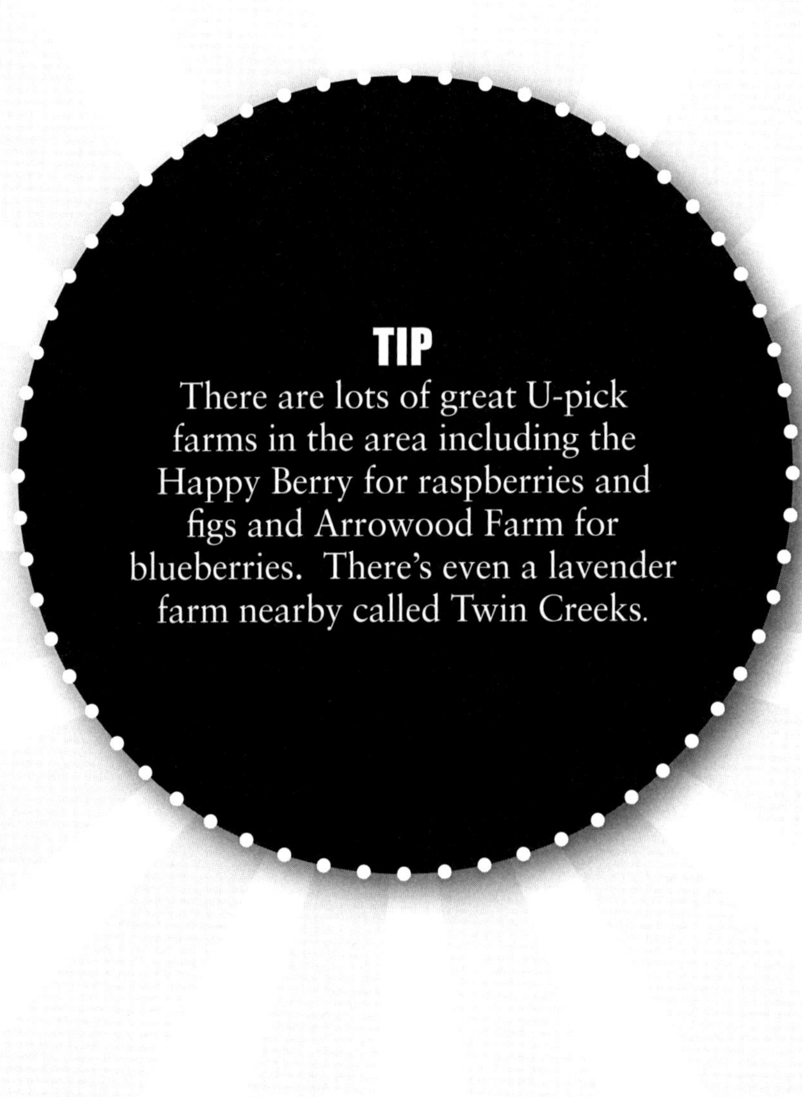

TIP

There are lots of great U-pick farms in the area including the Happy Berry for raspberries and figs and Arrowood Farm for blueberries. There's even a lavender farm nearby called Twin Creeks.

57

RIDE THE TROLLEY
THROUGH DOWNTOWN

The history of trolley transit in Greenville dates to the 20th century; an electric trolley began running in 1901. It could reach speeds of up to eight miles an hour and traversed Main Street. The tracks extended to nearby neighborhoods such as Overbrook within a decade, but by World War II trolleys were considered an inefficient mode of public transportation. Today, the red-and-blue-painted trolleys that run through downtown and into some of its most historic neighborhoods are open-air buses that can carry 35 people at a time. They have bike racks and are wheelchair accessible. It's a really fun way to get your first glimpse of Greenville, to get the lay of the land. They run year-round on Friday evenings, and all day Saturday and Sunday. It's an especially good way to get to Greenville Drive games or just a nice place to sit while enjoying an ice cream from Spill the Beans or Blueberry Frog.

greenvillesc.gov/597/Trolley

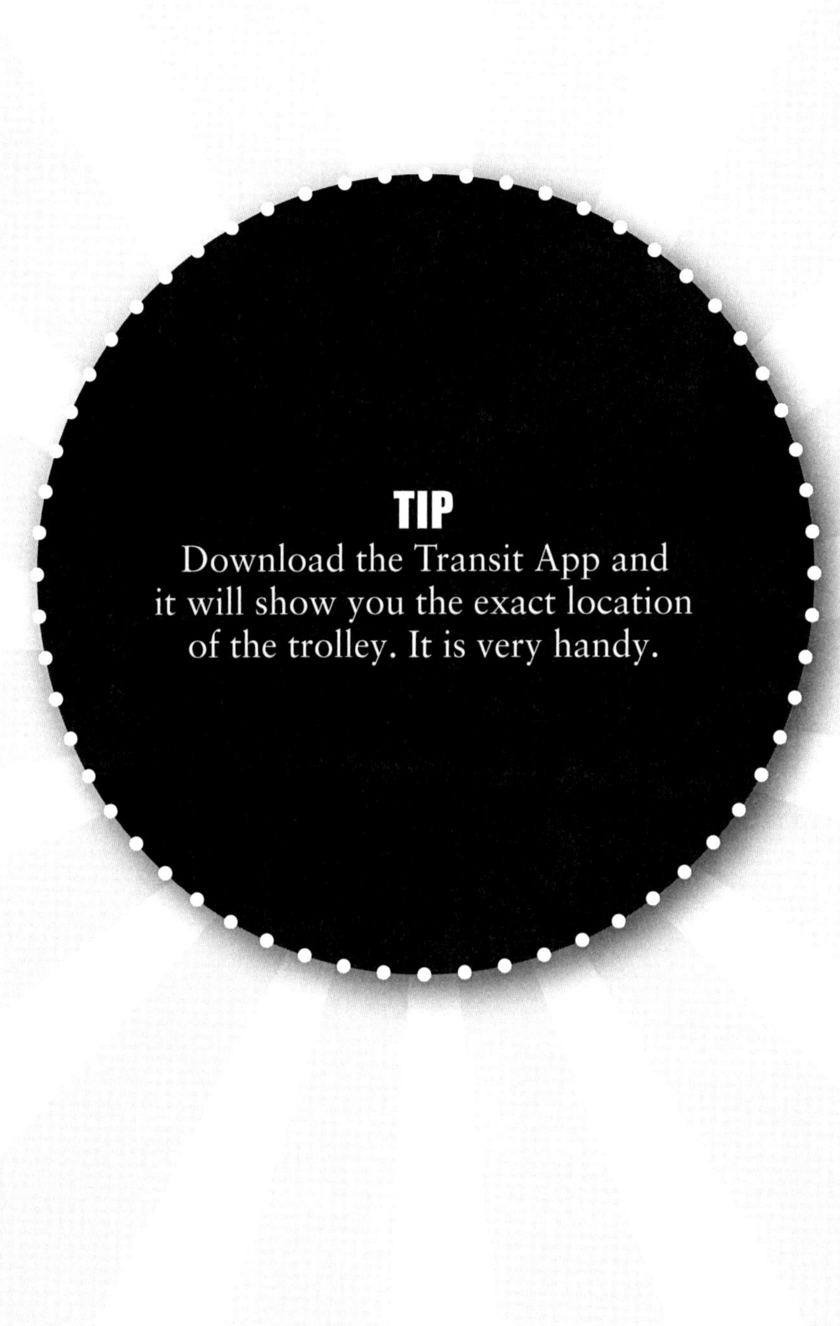
TIP
Download the Transit App and
it will show you the exact location
of the trolley. It is very handy.

58

EXPERIENCE THE THRILL
OF THE GREENVILLE SWAMP RABBITS

Hockey might not be the first thing that comes to mind when you think of Greenville, but the Greenville Swamp Rabbits deliver high-energy, fast-paced action that will make you an immediate fan. As a proud member of the ECHL and affiliate of the LA Kings (NHL) and Ontario Reign (AHL), the Swamp Rabbits bring the excitement to every game at Bon Secours Wellness Arena from October through April. Enjoy themed nights like Waggin' Wednesdays, where fans can bring their dogs, and the heartwarming charity Teddy Bear Toss. Whether you're a hardcore hockey fan or simply looking for a fun family night out, the Swamp Rabbits offer an unforgettable experience. Check the schedule, grab your tickets, and join the roar of the crowd!

650 N Academy St., 864-241-3800
swamprabbits.com

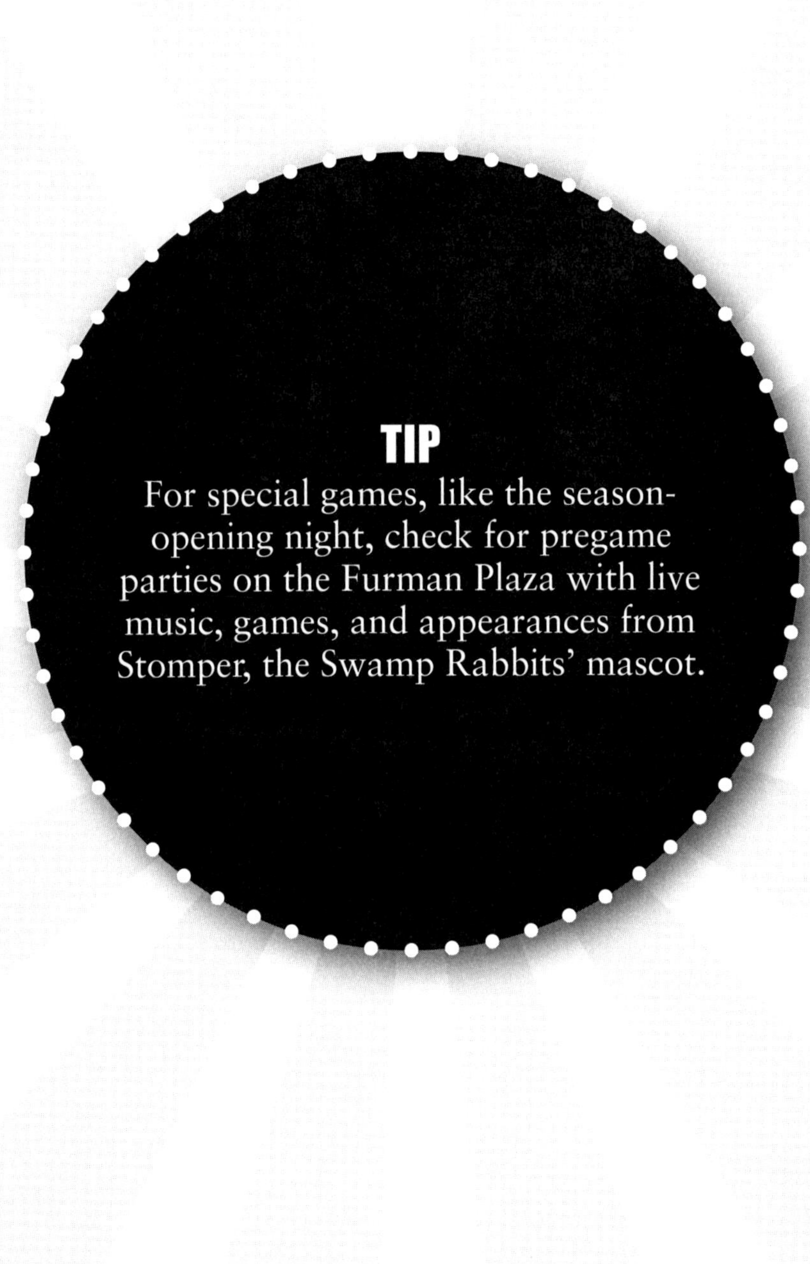

TIP

For special games, like the season-opening night, check for pregame parties on the Furman Plaza with live music, games, and appearances from Stomper, the Swamp Rabbits' mascot.

59

HIT THE GREENS
AT FURMAN UNIVERSITY

The Furman Golf Club is part of the university's campus and is open to the public. It's a par 72 course across 170 acres and was designed in the late 1950s by Richard K. Webel and Walter Cosby but renovated in 2008 to meet USGA specifications. Notably Beth Daniel and Dottie Pepper played here. There are stunning views of the Blue Ridge Mountains, wide, tree-lined fairways, and several lakes. The course layout has been referred to as challenging yet playable, with fast greens. The price to get on the course, even on a weekend, is less than $100, and locals like to get in nine holes on a weekday afternoon for just $28. The course is nearly playable year-round because of Greenville's mild winters. The club also has a driving range, putting greens, and a chipping area, as well as lessons and clinics for all ages.

400 N Hwy. 25 Byp., 864-294-2690
furmangolfclub.com

SHOW YOUR HOMETOWN PRIDE
WITH THE GREENVILLE TRIUMPH

The Greenville Triumph Soccer Club made history by becoming Upstate South Carolina's first professional team, igniting a wave of excitement among soccer fans. The Triumph's 2020 inaugural season culminated in a championship win, solidifying their position as a top contender in USL League One. Experience the electrifying atmosphere at a packed Paladin Stadium at Furman University, where the Reedy River Riot fan club creates a sea of green and gold. Truly, every Triumph match feels like a thrilling spectacle. More than just a team, the Triumph have become a source of community pride, uniting fans young and old across Upstate. In 2026, the Triumph will move to a state-of-the-art facility in Mauldin at BridgeWay Station, a mixed-use development filled with restaurants, bars, and interesting retail, ensuring the continued success of the club. Don't miss the opportunity to catch a game and be a part of the Triumph's journey.

22 S Main St., 864-203-0565
greenvilletriumph.com

61

CHEER ON THE CLEMSON TIGERS
AT MEMORIAL STADIUM

Being a part of the vibe at a Clemson football game is a true Upstate experience. Fans are passionate and they get decked out in orange and tiger print. Memorial Stadium holds 81,000-plus fans and is known as a loud, electric stadium experience. Right before the game starts, players touch Howard's Rock and run down the hill onto the field. It came from Death Valley in the 1960s and was given to Coach Frank Howard by Sam Jones. Howard is famously known for saying, "Give me 110 percent or keep your filthy hands off of my rock." Tailgating is a slice of South Carolina life at Clemson. The fields all around the stadium are packed with serious tailgating setups including RVs with live broadcast TVs, tents, grills, coolers, and lots of cornhole. If you want to explore the town of Clemson, famous spots to stop into include the Esso Club, Tiger Town Tavern, and Mac's Drive-In.

200 Champion Ave., Clemson, 864-656-3311
clemsontigers.com

62

BIKE LIKE THE PROS
AT HOTEL DOMESTIQUE

Inspired by the world travels of professional cyclist George Hincapie, Hotel Domestique is a boutique resort offering luxurious stays, exceptional cuisine, and unmatched outdoor experiences. It lies between Greenville and Asheville in the foothills of the Blue Ridge Mountains. The destination is a haven for cycling enthusiasts and adventure seekers. Guests can rent Ventum NS1 and GS1 bikes, custom fitted for each rider. Daily rentals include a Garmin 810, preloaded with Hincapie's favorite training routes. Whether you're riding solo or need a guide to match your pace, Hotel Domestique offers expert-led tours for every skill level. If you follow them on "Ride with GPS," you can ride the very routes Hincapie trained on throughout his career. Don't miss Gran Fondo Hincapie, a multiday cycling celebration featuring scenic rides, live music, and a family-friendly festival with food, drinks, and more. Join cycling pros, celebrities, and weekend warriors for an unforgettable ride through the Blue Ridge Parkway.

10 Road of Vines, Travelers Rest, 864-947-4083
hoteldomestique.com

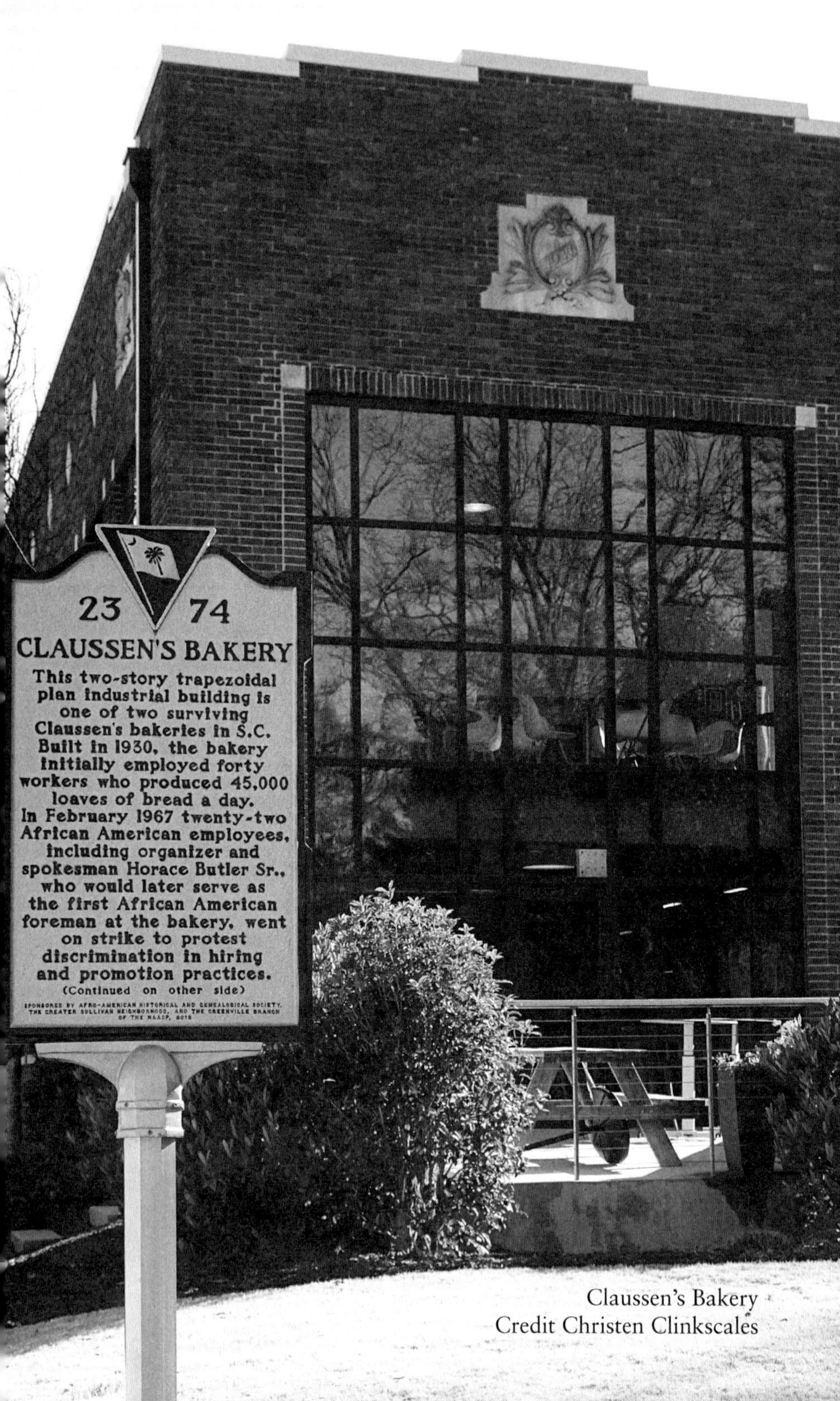

Claussen's Bakery
Credit Christen Clinkscales

CULTURE AND HISTORY

63

STAND WHERE
THE CLAUSSEN BAKERY STRIKE OCCURRED

The building at 400 Augusta Street is super special. The Claussen Bakery Strike occurred here in 1967, and Dr. Martin Luther King Jr. spoke in support of equal pay and promotion for the 22 striking employees. More than 3,000 people heard him say, "They had been called boys, then they stood up like men." The NAACP in Greenville called for a boycott of Claussen baked goods in response. Reverend Jesse Jackson was the director of Operation Breadbasket and played a big role in making the strike nationally noticed. In 2017, a historical marker was placed on-site honoring this moment in the civil rights movement. The Claussen Bakery Building today is home to an architecture firm, McMillan Pazdan Smith, and up until recently a brewery was in its basement. For civil rights era historians, this is hallowed ground.

400 Augusta St.
greenbookofsc.com/locations/claussen-bakery

CLIMB THE CAMPANILE
AT FURMAN UNIVERSITY

The bell tower is a symbol of the university and stands proudly at one end of Swan Lake on campus. It's an iconic structure, standing 58 feet tall, and is an example of Southern Gothic architecture. It is referred to as the Campanile. It has carved pediments, and its clock chimes on the hour and can play melodies, thanks to a 49-bell carillon. It is a replica of the bell tower built in 1854 that stood on the original Furman campus, which is now the Governor's School for the Arts at Falls Park downtown. This modern edifice was dedicated in 1963 to Furman's first president, Charles Ezra Daniel. At the top you'll find fantastic views of the campus, its lake, and the greater Paris Mountain area. Its brick exterior features arched windows and a copper weathervane. Check Furman's website for times that visitors can climb to the top.

3300 Poinsett Hwy., 864-294-2000
furman.edu

TIP

Furman is a wonderful place to bring a picnic lunch, but refrain from feeding the ducks or the swans; they are managed by their own caregivers.

EXPERIENCE ART
IN PUBLIC PLACES

The City of Greenville has a commission called Art in Public Places, and its collection of 120-plus permanent works installed throughout the city is posted online with walking directions and useful story maps. It's broken up into three categories: murals, statues, and structures, which are things that don't depict figures, including architectural elements and historic pieces. The commission is composed of nine members, and they convene monthly to plan and fund art initiatives. Notable works include the Rose Crystal Tower by Dale Chihuly and the statue of Peg Leg Bates by Joseph B. Thompson. The crown jewel of Art in Public Places is Guido van Helten's massive mural on the Canvas Tower, commissioned to commemorate the 50th anniversary of the desegregation of Greenville's schools. It is eight stories tall and spans more than 18,000 square feet. It is a photorealistic work featuring Greenville educator Pearlie Harris surrounded by AJ Whittenberg Elementary School students.

The Van Helten Mural
301 College St.

Art in Public Places Commission
greenvillesc.gov/1233/Arts-in-Public-Places-Commission

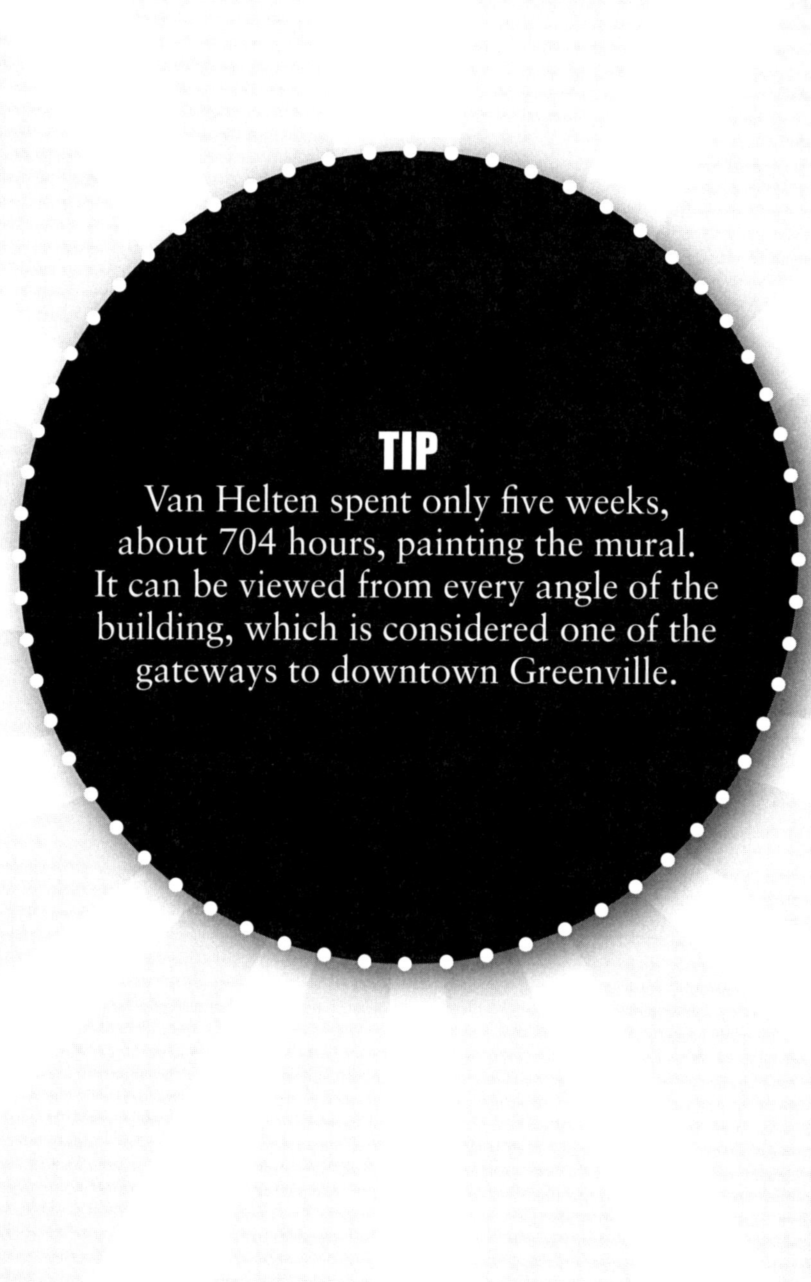

TIP

Van Helten spent only five weeks, about 704 hours, painting the mural. It can be viewed from every angle of the building, which is considered one of the gateways to downtown Greenville.

EXPERIENCE AN AWARD-WINNING CHILDREN'S MUSEUM

Covering 80,000 square feet in an afternoon might sound like a chore, but it's a whole lotta fun at the Children's Museum of the Upstate. There are interactive exhibits for the youngest to the simply young at heart. Hands-on activities in the areas of science, tech, engineering, the arts, and math encourage kids to discover via play. There's a life-size dino skeleton to maneuver and a plexiglass jungle maze to climb. It was one of the first children's museums to receive Smithsonian Affiliate status, awarded to the museum in 2014. This designation ensures that the museum reflects standards of the Smithsonian to increase and diffuse knowledge through its programming. The exhibits all have adorable names too, like Marsh Music, Reedy River Bend, the Upside Down, and SEAsations. There is a healthy café on-site and things to do outside. The building was originally Greenville County's main library and was reimagined for the museum.

300 College St., 864-233-7755
tcmupstate.org

OTHER GREAT PLACES TO HANG OUT WITH YOUR KIDS

South Carolina Children's Theatre
153 Augusta St., 864-235-2885
scchildrenstheatre.org

Hughes Main Library
25 Heritage Green Pl., 864-242-5000
greenvillelibrary.org/locations/main

Cancer Survivors Park
52 Cleveland St., 864-255-5010
cancersurvivorspark.org

North Main Rotary Park
9 Ashley Ave., 864-467-4355
greenvillesc.gov/1587/North-Main-Rotary-Park

Treetop Quest
2700 W Blue Ridge Dr., 864-907-9539
staging.treetopquest.com/greenville

67

GO WHERE THE GALLERIES ARE IN WEST GREENVILLE

West Greenville is often referred to as the city's arts district, though in fact Greenville is teaming with studios and galleries. But West Greenville is home to some fantastic ones including the one that started it all: Artbomb Studios. Artist Diane Kilgore formed a collective of studios for working artists, and they throw open their doors for a big show twice a year. There is also the studio of Joseph Bradley and his adjacent Spoon Bill Gallery. There is a stunning koi fishpond here in their walled garden. Sunny Mullarkey McGowan has a studio in the neighborhood too, as do ceramics artists Darin R. Gehrke and dozens more. Greenville Center of Creative Arts is in the historic Brandon Mill in West Greenville; it features rotating exhibits in its main gallery that are open to the public as well as hosts a slew of art classes and events.

villagewgvl.com

VISIT A CHURCH FULL OF ARTISTS

AT OYÉ STUDIOS

In 2019, artists Rey Alfonso and Patricia DeLeon along with Genna and Signe Grushovenko saved a former church from demolition to create a sanctuary of studios for working artists. The North Main structure on East Hillcrest is a sought-after space to create within, and it houses the studios of a dozen resident artists including Michelle Jardines, Jessica Fields, Glory Day Loflin, Christopher Rico, Dorothy Shain, and others. It is in one of Greenville's oldest neighborhoods, filled with hundred-year-old oak trees and a variety of architecture. The name Oyé is the Spanish word for "listen up," and it embodies the spirit of the church-turned-studios. The collective, as they like to think of themselves, hosts group shows and creates gallery spaces to share. There is something for every aesthetic at Oyé, from landscapes to pop art, abstracts to realism. Oyé is one of the top stops on the annual Open Studios tour, hosted by the Metropolitan Arts Council every fall.

37 E Hillcrest Dr.
oyestudiosgvl.com

WALK ACROSS
THE POINSETT BRIDGE

A feat of early engineering, the Poinsett Bridge is South Carolina's oldest and most historic surviving bridge. It was finished in 1820 as part of the State Road, which connected Charleston to Asheville. It spans Little Gap Creek, a tributary of Lake Jocassee. It is believed that Charleston native Robert Mills designed it; he is known for designing the Washington Monument. The Poinsett Bridge stands out for its 14-foot Gothic arch and 130-foot span. It was built without mortar and is comprised of locally quarried stone cut on-site. The bridge is a bit hard to locate and, even today, cell service is spotty in the Poinsett Bridge Heritage Preserve area. The best way to navigate there is to get directions to Camp Old Indian, a Boy Scout camp. The bridge is right next to it. It was added to the National Register of Historic Places in 1970 and is one of my very favorite places in all of the Upstate.

Callahan Mountain Rd.
nationalregister.sc.gov

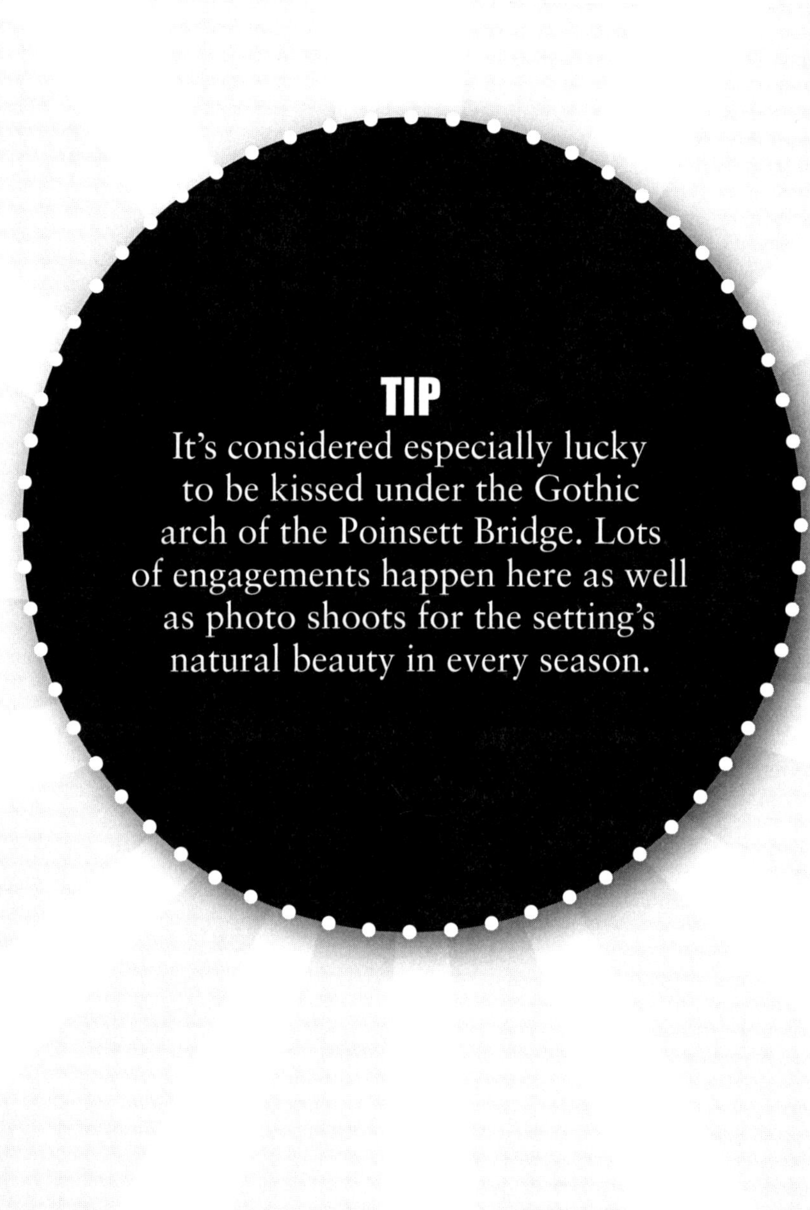

TIP

It's considered especially lucky to be kissed under the Gothic arch of the Poinsett Bridge. Lots of engagements happen here as well as photo shoots for the setting's natural beauty in every season.

EXPLORE FALLS PARK
AND THE LIBERTY BRIDGE

Greenville would be very different without a project that uncovered the natural waterfalls on the Reedy River, creating one of the nation's most celebrated urban parks. The Liberty Bridge was completed in 2004. It curves around the falls, suspended 345 feet in the air, and is for pedestrian traffic only. Its shape has become a symbol of the city, and even locals find time to enjoy it year-round. Falls Park is gorgeously landscaped with both naturalized spaces and highly curated planted beds. There are shelters and stages and swings and benches, and lots of green space to enjoy too. The riverbeds and adjacent areas have interesting textile ruins, some specifically from Vardry Mill, and though the river appears clean, it is not advised to play in the water because of its manufacturing past. Shakespeare in the Park happens here, and don't forget to visit the Medusa Tree; its exposed roots create a work of art you'll want to photograph.

601 S Main St., 864-467-4355
greenvillesc.gov/175/Liberty-Bridge

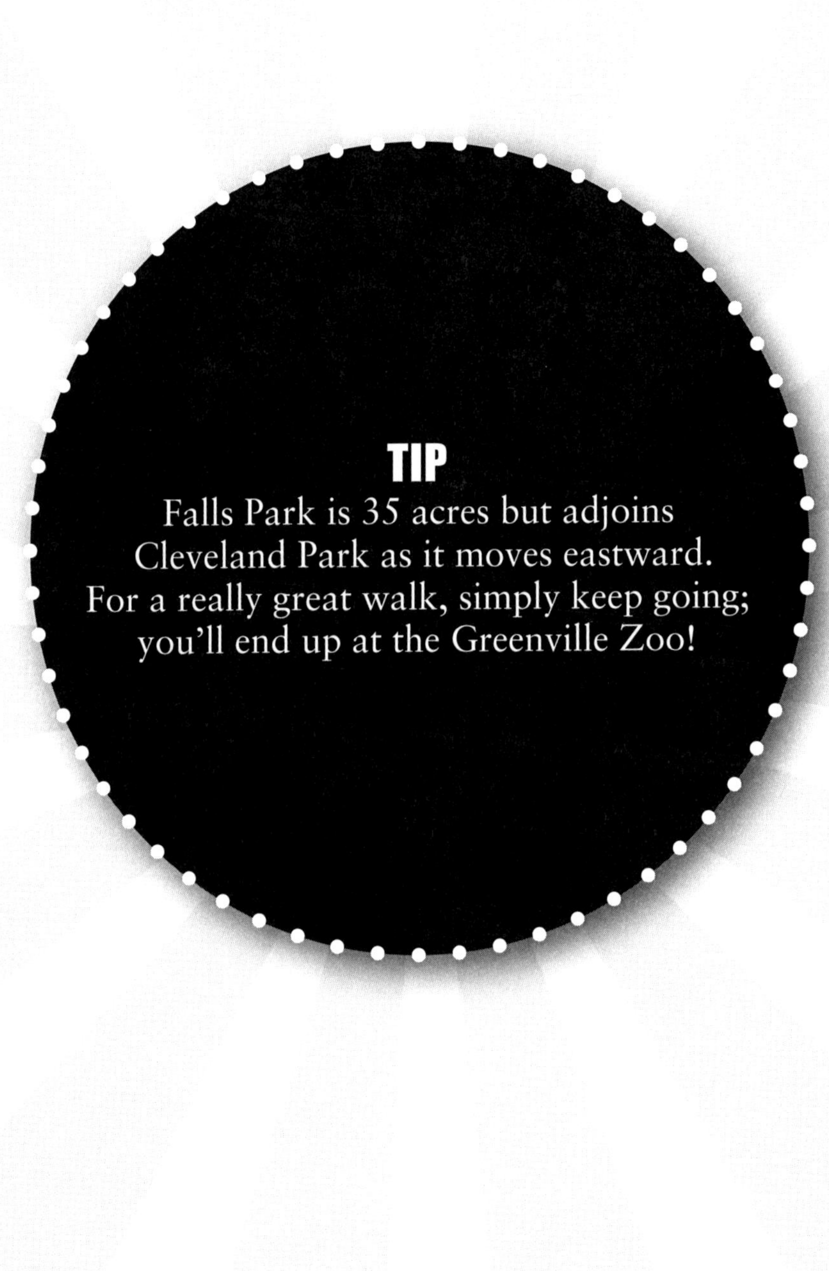
TIP
Falls Park is 35 acres but adjoins Cleveland Park as it moves eastward. For a really great walk, simply keep going; you'll end up at the Greenville Zoo!

71

LEARN SOMETHING NEW
AT THE
UPCOUNTRY HISTORY MUSEUM

Explore the rich history of the region at the Upcountry History Museum right on the Heritage Green campus. It's affiliated with Furman University and offers a mix of rotating Southern exhibits and also maintains a permanent collection. The reason for being is the history of what we call the Upcountry including Native American and Colonial history and up to the Civil War. This era includes Greenville's significant textile history. The museum also hosts national traveling shows that have featured World War II and the civil rights movement, even pop culture. There are vintage pieces, textiles, artifacts, and interesting documents. It's all brought to life via docents, educational programming, and guest lectures. If you're lucky enough to be invited to an event here, accept! The museum throws an amazing party among its fascinating setting.

540 Buncombe St., 864-467-3100
upcountryhistory.org

72

TAKE A WALK

WITH GREENVILLE HISTORY TOURS

John Nolan is Greenville's most beloved modern historian, and the tours he offers with Greenville History Tours are exceptional. There are driving and walking tours and seasonal ones too. During the fall, you can walk through both of Greenville's exceptionally historic graveyards downtown. He will delve into Greenville's storied past, identifying historic trends and, at times, gentrification of its neighborhoods. He's been featured in publications like National Geographic Traveler and Southern Living. Beloved neighborhoods include North Main and Hampton Pinckney. John also offers signature tours surrounding food and beverage. Called "At the Chef's Table," his culinary tour features some of Greenville's best restaurants and outstanding chefs. He also hosts a BBQ Trail driving tour that canvases two to three hours of barbecue joints.

206 S Main St., 864-567-3940
greenvillehistorytours.com

STROLL
HISTORIC EARLE STREET

The Colonel Elias Earle Historic District Association is a mouthful to say, but it encompasses some of Greenville's most spectacular historic homes along a one-mile stretch. The district includes both Earle Street and James Street, where many textile owners built their family homes. It was named for Elias Earle, who at one time owned most of the North Main neighborhood. It was designated a national historic district in 1982 for homes built between 1915 and 1930 including fine examples of Federal and Georgian homes, Tudor and Colonial Revival, and Bungalow-Craftsman design. But the big reason you may want to stroll down Earle Street is for its holiday exuberance. This is where thousands of trick-or-treaters descend on October 31. Door knocking begins at 5 p.m. and is over by 9 p.m.; many residents spend hundreds of dollars on candy and decor. At Christmas, more than 70 homes inflate identical Santas in their yards, creating a red and white lane of joy.

greenvillesc.gov/526/Colonel-Elias-Earle-Historic-District

The summer home of Governor Henry Middleton is here, called Whitehall; it was built in 1813. Look for the historic marker near the sidewalk at 310 West Greenville to learn more, but please don't knock. It remains a private home.

STAY
AT THE POINSETT HOTEL

Today it's the Westin Poinsett, but for decades it was known as The Poinsett Hotel. It was named for Joel Poinsett, a South Carolina politician and the first minister to Mexico. In fact, the poinsettia flower in the US is named after him. It opened in 1925 and was called "The Million Dollar Hotel," though in fact it cost $1.5 million to erect. It was designed by famed New York architect William Lee Stoddart, known for his expertise in Beaux-Arts design. It offered 248 rooms and was one of the tallest buildings in Greenville at the time. Amelia Earhart stayed here, as did John Barrymore and Bobby Kennedy, but it faced hard times in the 1970s and closed for decades. It reopened in October 2000 to much fanfare after an extensive and historically accurate renovation. It was honored by Historic Hotels of America in 2021 as the Best City Center Historic Hotel, and much of Greenville enjoyed spying George Clooney and Renée Zellweger here when they filmed the movie Leatherheads.

120 S Main St., 864-421-9700
marriot.com

FIND ALL
THE MICE ON MAIN

Main Street is a 10-block stretch that always seems to be growing. It was named a "Great American Main Street" by the National Trust for Historic Preservation for its tree-lined street, sidewalk cafés, diverse retail shops, and cultural stops. An art installation worth noticing is Mice on Main. It was inspired by the book Goodnight Moon and consists of bronze statues of mice by sculptor Zan Wells installed between the Hyatt Regency and the Westin Poinsett hotels. It was a senior project idea by Jim Ryan in 2000 and has become a beloved fixture for locals and visitors alike. Wells is the artist behind three other bronze sculptures on Main Street. You can see Joel Poinsett in front of M. Judson Booksellers. Dick Riley stands in the plaza of the Peace Center, and Charles Townes, inventor of the laser, sits across the street from the entrance to Falls Park.

miceonmain.com

TIP

Local stores, such as Mast General, have a list of clues to share if you need help locating all nine mice. Each figure holds a bit of whimsy that relates back to the bedtime story.

FALL INTO THE WORLD OF JASPER JOHNS

AT GREENVILLE COUNTY'S ART MUSEUM

There's an acclaimed collection of American art at the Greenville County Museum of Art. From federal portraits to the contemporary, there's something for every visitor, but two major collections really stand out: Andrew Wyeth and Jasper Johns. Before his death, Wyeth said that Greenville holds the best collection of his watercolors in any public museum. There are two dozen, highlighting his aptitude at painting landscapes and pastoral scenes of normalcy. The Jasper Johns collection is significantly larger, with 117 pieces including paintings in oil, acrylic, encaustic, and watercolor. There are also sculptures, drawings, and hand-produced prints. Johns is considered a substantive contemporary artist. Born in 1930, he spent his childhood in South Carolina. The Greenville collection includes works from surrealism to minimalism, conceptual art, and pop. Johns is celebrated for exploring personal themes through application, and the span of work at the Greenville County Museum of Art is a joy to visit.

420 College St., 864-271-7570
gcma.org

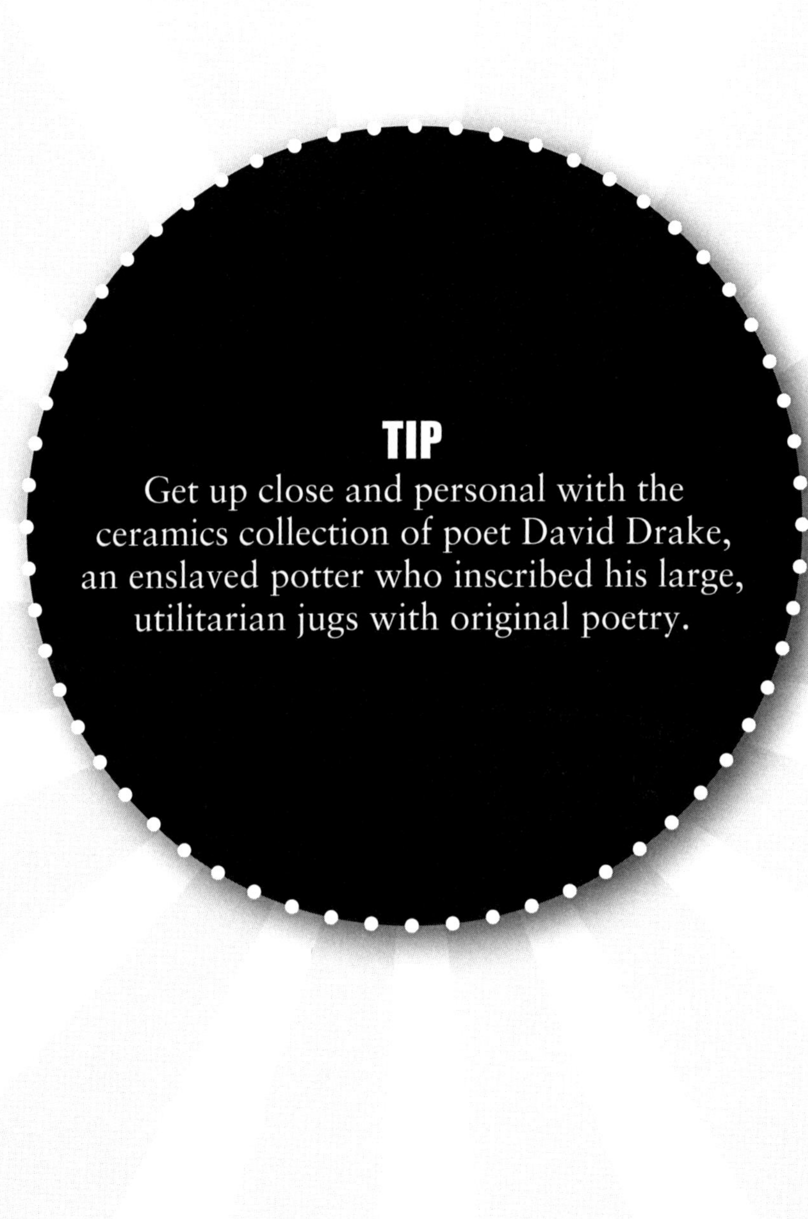

TIP

Get up close and personal with the ceramics collection of poet David Drake, an enslaved potter who inscribed his large, utilitarian jugs with original poetry.

77

CHECK OUT A REIMAGINED TEXTILE COMPLEX
AT THE TAYLORS MILL

Taylors is a bedroom community of Greenville that cropped up about the same time as downtown, around 1920. The Taylors Mill was originally Southern Bleachery and Piedmont Print Works. It played a big role in textile history in Greenville, focusing on bleaching, dyeing, or printing fabric milled by area companies. At one time it employed more than 1,000 workers, and its complex included a store, a mill village, rec facilities, sports teams, a health center, and housing, as well as centers of worship. It stood vacant for decades, but around 2015 redevelopment efforts reimagined the Taylors Mill as a place for artist studios, offices, events, coffee shops, and other restaurants. The Farehouse is here, as are 13 Stripes Brewery and Junto Coffee. It's a great example of adaptive reuse and is really something to explore.

250 Mill St., 864-335-9913
taylorsmill.community

TIP

If you visit Greenville for MAC Open Studios, you'll get to visit many local artists.

GO TO THE
BMW ZENTRUM

This one-of-a-kind facility showcases the history of BMW, both as a brand and its storied place manufacturing in the Upstate. Called the Zentrum, it's both a museum of innovation and a visitors center for driving enthusiasts. There are interactive displays, as well as mint-condition vehicles of all eras, engines, and auto technology to ogle. Consider adding on a production tour, which is guided and a load of fun for all ages; you get to watch a BMW be built from beginning to end. There's a gift store, of course, and plenty of spots to take photos and portraits. The BMW Driving Experience is by reservation only and is a pricey ticket, but participants get to learn how to drive like a race car driver and maneuver situational obstacles in real time. And, yes, you get to go really, really fast on the racetrack or let a driver take you for a lap.

1400 Hwy. 101, Greer, 864-802-6000
bmwgroup-werke.com

VISIT ONE OF THE OLDEST BUILDINGS IN THE UPSTATE AT HANS & FRANZ

Located just off Highway 14, Hans & Franz is a brick building complex dating to the Civil War era, though some locals believe it to be much older. Purportedly built in 1862, the main mill structure is among the oldest in Greenville. It was once used to sew uniforms, and possibly to house munitions. Since 2014 it's been a German-style biergarten imagined by Addy Sulley. The jovial restaurateur recently passed away and is missed by his many regulars. He spent two years extensively renovating it and preserving many of its original features. The menu is a fantastic mix of Bavarian dishes, and they offer lots of German beer. The indoor and outdoor spaces make Hans & Franz a fun spot to go with a group, especially on Friday nights when lots of locals meet up, like local celebrity and media host Jay Spivey. Oktoberfest is a fun time to visit Hans & Franz; the bar really goes all out.

3124 S Hwy. 14, 864-627-8263
hansandfranzbiergarten.net

WALK THE CAMPUS
OF THE SC GOVERNOR'S SCHOOL FOR THE ARTS

Greenville has a boarding school dedicated to the performing arts for high school juniors and seniors. The campus is in the same location as Furman University's original location. Today this is part of Falls Park, and, in fact, its library has the most stunning view of both the Liberty Bridge and the waterfalls of the Reedy River. It was established by Virginia Uldrich in 1999 and is available to all South Carolina students, offered by audition. It is tuition-free and focuses on apprenticeship-style learning from nationally acclaimed professionals in the areas of creative writing, dance, film and drama, music, and visual arts. The campus feels like a hamlet of buildings and flower beds, and the exterior is open for a public stroll. Check the high school's calendar for public performances around Greenville as well as end-of-semester events and end-of-year performances, which are stellar and often free.

15 University St., 864-282-3777
scgsah.org

Augusta Twenty
Credit Christen Clinkscales

SHOPPING AND FASHION

81

TAKE A COOKING CLASS
AT THE COOK'S STATION

Part gourmet market, part kitchen store, part cooking school, part café, the Cook's Station is a Greenville institution and well worth an afternoon. If you can't find it at the Cook's Station for your kitchen, then it probably doesn't exist. Shelves are stocked with specialty products from local and regional purveyors as well as with items sourced from around the world. There are tools; there's wine, cheese, and snacks; there's cookware; and we haven't even scratched the surface of the prepared food offerings. Upstairs are classrooms to learn or to simply watch and taste. Classes range from fine-dining cooking to sushi, cast-iron cooking, baking, and classes for kids, adults, date nights, girls' nights out, and more. The heated covered patio is a fun place to hang out solo or with a group. Charcuterie boards are lovingly composed, and wines by the glass offer a nice selection.

515 Buncombe St., 864-250-0091
thecooksstation.com

STEP INTO LILLY PULITZER HQ

AT PINK BEE

A Greenville institution for over 20 years, Pink Bee GVL started as Bumble Bees, a beloved children's boutique, before transforming into a premier Lilly Pulitzer store. Now in its downtown location, Pink Bee has expanded even further, offering a carefully curated collection of national and international brands for all ages. Owner Tara Leary has created a shopping experience that blends classic, colorful style with modern sophistication. Whether you're looking for the perfect sundress, a statement accessory, or timeless outerwear, you'll find standout pieces from brands like Longchamp, Barbour, Vineyard Vines, and Smith & Quinn. Step inside and explore Pink Bee's sun-drenched world, where each piece is selected with style and quality in mind. Whether you're a longtime Lilly lover or discovering Pink Bee for the first time, you're sure to find something bright, bold, and expressive.

105 Augusta St., 864-271-4332
pinkbeegvl.com

TIP

Find easy parking right behind the store on University Street.

83

UNLEASH YOUR INNER KID

AT O.P. TAYLOR'S

Downtown Greenville's O.P. Taylor's isn't just a toy store, it's an experience. Proudly calling itself the "coolest toy store on the planet," this independent shop is a wonderland packed with classic games, modern must-haves, and an unbeatable selection of educational toys. LEGO lovers take note: O.P. Taylor's boasts an impressive lineup, including hard-to-find retired sets, making it a must-visit for collectors and builders. Beyond LEGO, you'll find treasures from brands like Cobi, Pokémon, Melissa & Doug, and Squishmallow, ensuring something special for kids and kids-at-heart. But the magic doesn't stop at the shelves. The friendly, knowledgeable staff are always ready to help, making every visit feel like playtime. Whether you're shopping for a gift, indulging in nostalgia, or discovering something new, O.P. Taylor's is a magical stop where fun has no age limit.

117 N Main St., 864-467-1984
optaylors.com

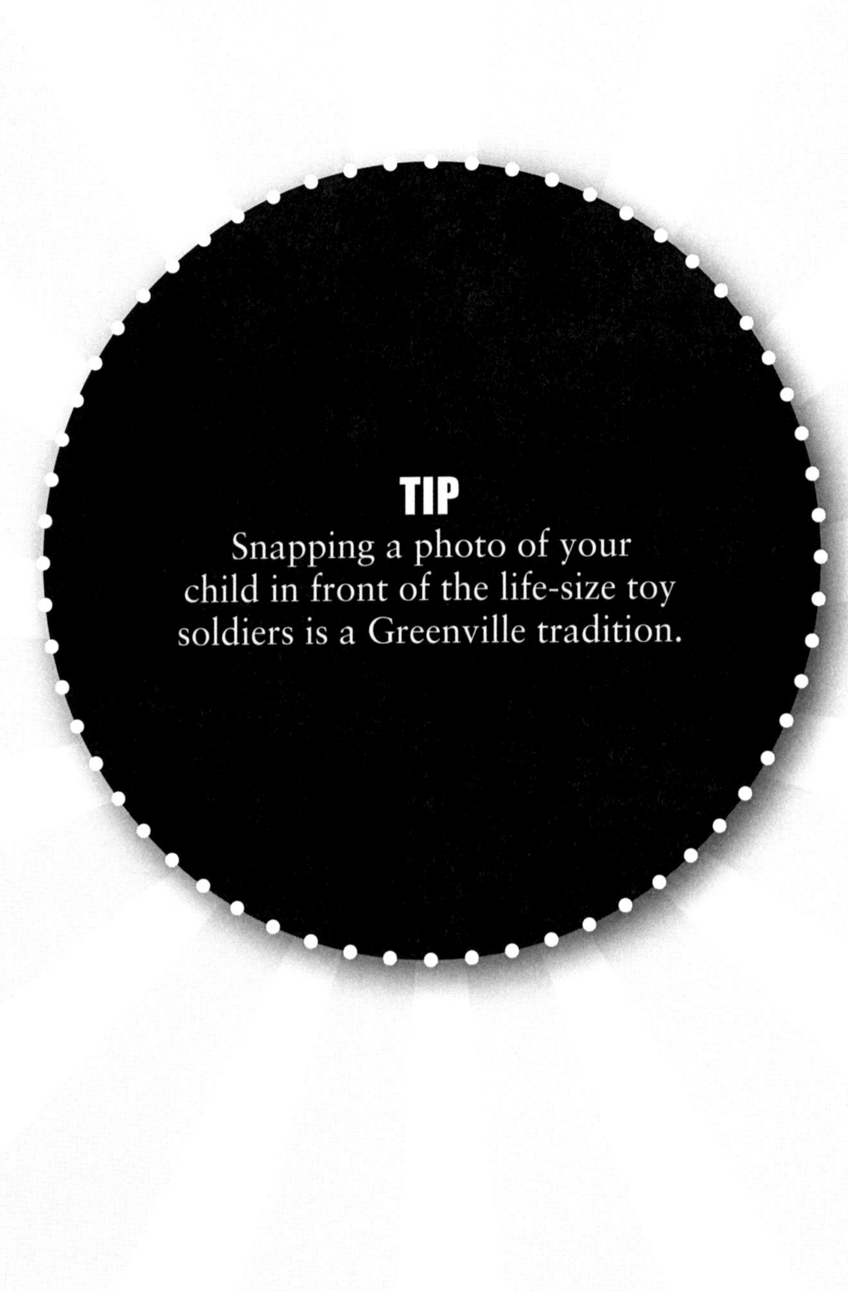
TIP
Snapping a photo of your child in front of the life-size toy soldiers is a Greenville tradition.

DRESS TO IMPRESS
AT AUGUSTA TWENTY

Located in Greenville's Historic West End, Augusta Twenty has been a fashion destination for more than two decades, offering curated, contemporary pieces designed for timeless wear. This thoughtfully curated boutique carries coveted brands like Mother Denim, Enza Costa, Rag & Bone, and Ulla Johnson, making it a go-to for style mavens. Beyond fashion, Augusta Twenty offers personalized service, a beverage bar, gourmet baked goods, and handpicked gifts. After browsing, cozy up next door at A20 Café, where you can sip a morning coffee or an afternoon glass of wine in its truly charming setting. Relax in a cozy spot surrounded by unique finds like candles, glassware, and linens, adding to the boutique's effortlessly chic vibe. With its inviting atmosphere, expertly curated selections, and elevated shopping experience, Augusta Twenty is a West End favorite for those who love fashion and a touch of everyday luxury.

26 Augusta St., 864-354-5857
augustatwenty.com

85

EXPERIENCE TIMELESS STYLE AND UNMATCHED SERVICE AT RUSH WILSON

Rush Wilson Limited has been a cornerstone of Greenville's menswear scene since 1950, delivering a refined shopping experience for discerning gentlemen. This establishment is well known for exceptional service and collections of classic, high-end clothing and footwear. From formal attire to stylish casual wear, Rush Wilson offers a range of options from brands such as Peter Millar, H. Goose, johnnie-O, and Armin Oehler. The store's signature is its custom clothing service, where they craft bespoke suits, sport coats, trousers, and shirts tailored to individual tastes. Whether you're searching for suiting for a special occasion, a sport coat to elevate your everyday look, or a pert shirt-and-tie combination, the staff at Rush Wilson provides expert guidance and ensures a one-of-a-kind personalized shopping experience. With a commitment to quality and a refined selection of menswear, Rush Wilson Limited remains a Greenville institution for those who appreciate craftsmanship.

23 W North St., 864-232-2761
rushwilson.com

86

CELEBRATE THE HANDMADE
AT INDIE CRAFT PARADE

Each September, the Makers Collective hosts Indie Craft Parade, a craft and goods market of 100-plus juried vendors. The weekend festival has been held in historic locations around Greenville, including the Taylors Mill, the Huguenot Building, and Furman University. It's always fun to see what neat location the Makers Collective will pick next! With a focus on Southern artisans, Indie Craft Parade is known for its curated home goods, handmade gifts, artisanal food and beverage offerings, unique clothing and jewelry, and so much more. You'll spot buyers looking to stock their stores as well as beautiful people selecting discerning items. Brands with cult followings like Leaph Boutique, Annie Koelle, Once Again Sam, and Karen Schipper are often at Indie Craft Parade. An opening party on Friday is a fun ticketed event with demos, live entertainment, and greater access to connect with the makers.

makerscollective.org

CREATE YOUR OWN SCENT
AT GREENVILLE SOY CANDLE COMPANY

Step into Greenville Soy Candle Company, where the air is filled with the world's best-smelling scents and shelves are stocked with artisanal, handcrafted natural candles and soaps. More than just a shop, this downtown microfactory is home to expert chandlers who craft all-natural home fragrance and body products using soy wax, essential oils, and plant-based butters. Want to create your own? Join a candle-making class, held every weekend, where a chandler will guide you through scent selection, coloring, and ingredients as you pour your own custom candle. It is an unforgettable experience for ages 16 and up. Committed to using only the cleanest, most sustainable ingredients, Greenville Soy Candle Company ensures its products are good for your home, your body, and the planet. Stop by and discover why this scent shop is a must-visit for candle lovers.

209 N Main St. B, 864-520-2511
gvlsoycandle.com

TIP

The scent "Mistletoe" is the shop's seasonal bestseller.

88

DISCOVER UNIQUE TREASURES
AT URBAN DIGS

Just outside downtown Greenville, Urban Digs is a welcoming boutique filled with select gifts, home decor, houseplants, and local art. Discover the perfect gift for any occasion and budget, from modern and traditional to vintage and eclectic treasures. Owner Amy Walcher has created a space that feels like home, where every item feels unique. She definitely has a green thumb, offering the lushest selection of plants and terrariums. The shop features locally made goods from the area's talented artisans, ensuring that each visit brings new and unique finds for customers. Whether you're searching for the perfect housewarming gift, a new plant, or a one-of-a-kind vintage piece, there's always something fresh. And if you're lucky, you'll be greeted by Lily Mae, the beloved shop dog and Head of Customer Relations. You will always find the perfect gift here; stop by, explore, and take home a little Greenville charm.

215 Wade Hampton Blvd., 864-233-6821
urbandigsgreenville.com

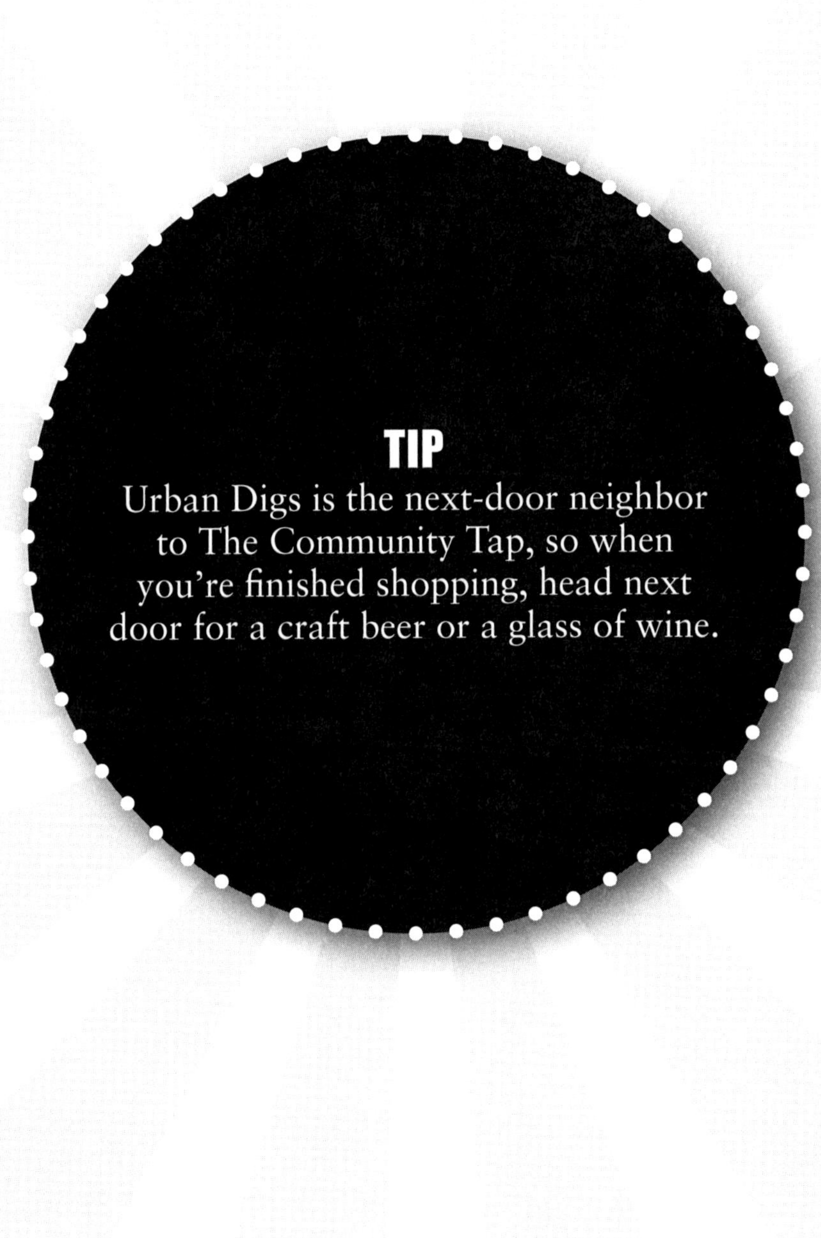

TIP

Urban Digs is the next-door neighbor to The Community Tap, so when you're finished shopping, head next door for a craft beer or a glass of wine.

SHOP TILL YOU DROP
AT THE NESTED FIG HOME AND THE NESTED FIG GARDEN

There's a duo on social media that has a huge following (like hundreds of thousands). Wesley Turner and Steven Merck are best friends and business partners, and following their antics about their stores in the Augusta Road area is truly delightful. The Nested Fig Home is a beautifully curated store; it includes furniture, decor, and tabletop and seasonal items. The Nested Fig Garden is an indoor oasis of houseplants and everything verdant you want in your home and on your patio. There's even a flower bar with local blooms from Wesley's husband's flower farm, called Petal Pickers. Wesley and Steven have a warm style that feels Southern chic but livable, and they've turned their two retail stores into an online experience of more than 1,500 items available at any one time. Their live sales are avidly followed, and getting to follow along while they shop the furniture and gift markets all over the country feels like an insider's coup.

The Nested Fig Home
3021 Augusta St., 864-991-3881, thenestedfighome.com

The Nested Fig Garden
2235 Augusta St., 864-241-0100, thenestedfiggarden.com

Or you can visit the guys online at thenestedfig.com

OTHER GREAT PLACES TO SHOP FOR GIFTS AND THE HOME

The Rock House Antiques
415 Mauldin Rd.
864-299-8981
therockhouseantiques.com

Artifacts Greenville
3209 Old Buncombe Rd.
864-569-2313
artifactsgreenville.com

Cottage Grove Vintage Market
1607 Laurens Rd.
864-423-9661
cottagegrovevintage.com

Ballard Designs Showroom
660 S Main St.
864-214-0572
ballarddesigns.com

Vintage Now Modern
633 S Main St.
864-385-5004
vintagenowmodern.com

Scarlet Tassel Gift & Home
27 S Pleasantburg Dr., Ste. 110
864-236-1969
scarlettassel.com

The Vintage at Main
13 E Coffee St., Ste. A
864-569-8237
thevintageatmain.com

Twigs
1100 Woods Crossing Rd.
864-297-6232
twigs.net

Sun and Soil Plant Parlor
403 Augusta St.
864-214-1288
sunandsoilplantparlor.com

The Vintage Market of Greenville
5500 Augusta Rd.
864-451-7042
facebook.com/GreenvilleAntiques20017

IMMERSE YOURSELF
AT THE GRAND BOHEMIAN GALLERY

After a day exploring Falls Park, step inside the gallery at the Grand Bohemian Hotel, where every piece has a story to tell. This gallery space, which is adjacent to the lobby, showcases an assortment of paintings, sculptures, and jewelry, featuring both local and emerging artists. With new pieces added frequently, the gallery offers a fresh experience with every visit. Whether you're a collector or simply browsing, you'll find stunning work inspired by the hotel's design. There are rotating exhibits too with featured artist such as Cuban painter Michelle Jardines, known for her dreamlike landscapes, and metal sculptor Yuri Tsuzuki. Every work is for sale, allowing you to bring the style of the hotel's interiors home. Stop by and discover something truly special at the Grand Bohemian Gallery. Grab a post-shopping drink downstairs at Spirit & Bower, their indoor/outdoor bar known for the cocktails, bourbon selection, and small plates.

44 E Camperdown Way, 864-520-5300
kesslercollection.com

TIP
Take a drink out to their outdoor firepit and enjoy four seasons of beautiful Greenville weather.

91

BECOME PART OF THE STORY AT M. JUDSON BOOKSELLERS

M. Judson Booksellers is more than a bookstore; it is a downtown literary hub in Greenville's historic courthouse building. You'll find shelves filled with bestsellers, poetry, Southern lit, cookbooks, and handpicked gift items sourced from across the Upstate. They also have a wonderful and celebrated children's and young adult section. The staff believes in the power of stories to connect and inspire, and they love to share their personal favorites with customers. Whether you're searching for your next great read or a unique gift, you'll find something special here. And don't forget to stop by Camilla Kitchen, located inside the store. Because books go best with coffee, wine, and tasty snacks, there's nothing better than pairing a good story with a delicious bite.

130 S Main St., 864-603-2412
mjudsonbooks.com

TIP

Try “Blind Date with a Book,” where the staff at M. Judson picks a favorite, wraps it in brown paper, and summarizes the plot on the front.

EXPERIENCE THOUGHTFUL FASHION
AT CUSTARD BOUTIQUE

At Custard Boutique, fashion is about more than just clothing; it's about embracing individuality in every customer. Located downtown in the South Main Street area, this thoughtful shop offers fashion-forward styles that complement every body shape, budget, and personality. Owner Tara Kirkland is passionate about local, eco-friendly, and purpose-driven fashion, and this tenet extends to accessories too. Shopping with Tara feels like browsing with your best friend. She effortlessly selects pieces, offers thoughtful suggestions, and makes every interaction feel like catching up with a chic bestie. The selection includes clothing, shoes, bags, jewelry, and gifts, each chosen with care and an eye for detail focusing on local artisans as much as possible. Look for the friendly Great Pyrenees shop dog, Azra, when you walk in. Custard is a welcoming space where every shopper is heard, respected, and appreciated.

718-A S Main St., 864-271-0927
custardboutique.com

93

SHOP LIKE AN INSIDER
AT THE WILSON GIRLS POP-UP

The Unity Park neighborhood was once filled with postwar cottages and peppered with corner stores. Sisters Cathleen Wilson Seay and Jean Wilson Freeman bought a long forgotten one and turned it into a space for their creative endeavors. Today, they invite the public in five times a year for several days in March, April, September, October, and early December. It's a curated shopping experience filled with art, home goods, select decor, favorite regional makers, jewelry, custom textiles, and vintage pieces hand-selected by the duo. Rest assured, if it wouldn't be in their own homes, it won't be for sale at Wilson Girls. Look for Jean's painted florals; she's a celebrated Southern artist. And Cathleen's "Salty Silver" comprised of rude phrases engraved on vintage silverplate. Each pop-up features wares from up to a dozen local artisans, including select seasonal decor, books, local flowers, and gourmet items. There are interesting furnishing and lamps too.

59 E Main St.
Instagram: @wilsongirlsllc

94

FIND INSTAGRAM-WORTHY STYLE
AT HARRINGTONS

Step into Harringtons, where the contemporary meets timeless wardrobe staples. Founded by Jenny Hall, a former fashion blogger with a devoted Instagram following, this boutique is a dream realized, and a carefully curated space designed to celebrate personal style. From everyday essentials to statement pieces, Harringtons carries a select mix of brands, including Alden Adair, Free People, Victoria Dunn, and Briton Court. This one-of-a-kind label was created by Jenny, her twin sister Stephe, and their sister Kristina. Harringtons is an elevated shopping experience, offering top service and truly warm hospitality. Whether you're building a wardrobe or adding fresh seasonal pieces, stop in, browse, and let Harringtons help you curate a wardrobe that makes you feel effortless. The store has parking right out front so it's easy to pop in and see what's new.

6 W Lewis Plz., 864-666-1814
shopharringtons.com

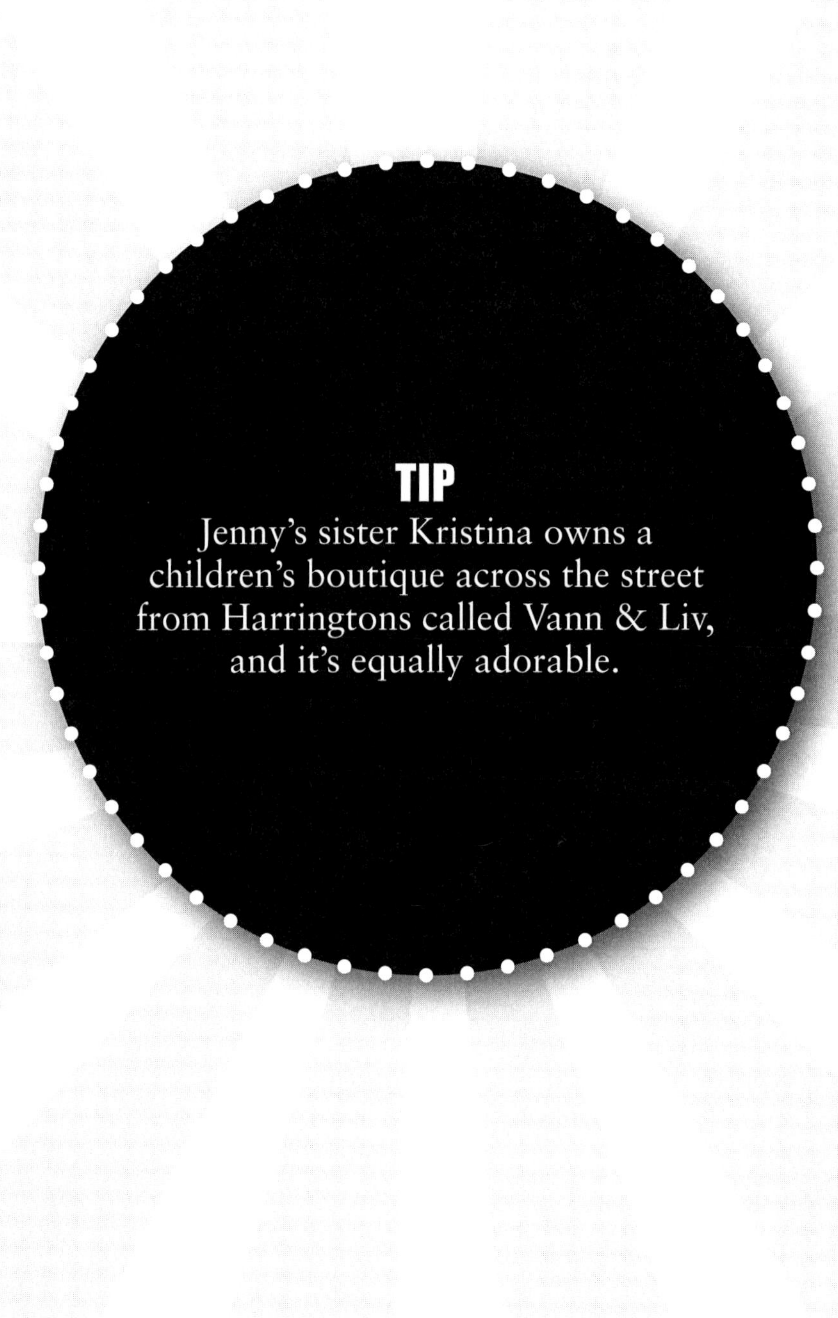
TIP
Jenny's sister Kristina owns a children's boutique across the street from Harringtons called Vann & Liv, and it's equally adorable.

95

STEP BACK IN TIME
AT MAST GENERAL STORE

Since 2003, Mast General Store has been a popular fixture on Main Street, welcoming visitors with its old-timey charm and variety of goods. Housed in a perfectly restored storefront, the interior's pressed-tin ceiling and warm maple flooring are something to see, creating the perfect setting for an emporium filled with nostalgia. Inside, find an impressive mix of clothing, outdoor gear, and knickknacks. Outdoorspeople will love the stocked outfitters department, featuring brands like the North Face, Columbia, Keen, and Kelty. The mercantile department is a trove of cast iron cookware, handcrafted soaps, pottery, books, and old-fashioned toys. Don't forget the candy section, boasting 500-plus varieties of classic treats. The service here is second to none, with happy employees ready to help. With its inviting atmosphere and curated selection, it's more than a shop; it's a destination. You will certainly find something special at Mast General Store to take home.

111 N Main St., 864-235-1883
mastgeneralstore.com

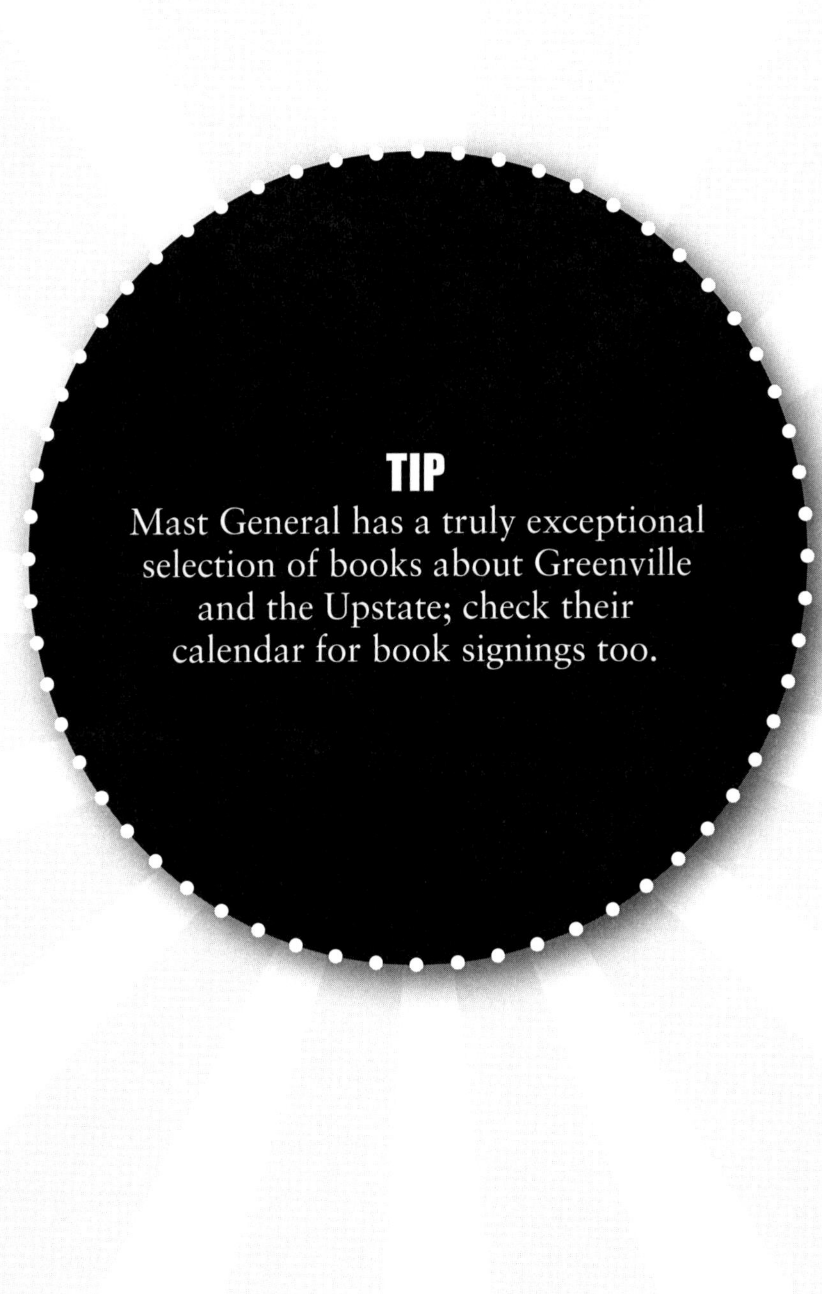
TIP
Mast General has a truly exceptional selection of books about Greenville and the Upstate; check their calendar for book signings too.

96

GET READY TO GET WET
AT SPLASH ON MAIN

Owner Anne Mayher created Splash on Main to be a go-to boutique for everything related to life on the water. Whether you're heading to an exotic beach, a lakeside retreat, or just lounging by the pool, Splash on Main offers a varied selection of swimwear, resort wear, and accessories. Here you can shop top swim brands like Citrine, L*Space, Shoshanna, Seafolly, and Miraclesuit, plus stylish clothing from THML, Pinch, and One Hundred Stars. From chic cover-ups to beach bags and sunscreen, Splash on Main has everything you need to soak up the sun in style. Their friendly staff and attentive team will help you find the perfect fit, no matter your size or budget, and feel great about your next sun-drenched adventure.

807 S Main St., 864-534-1510
splashonmain.com

TIP

Splash on Main is known for their amazing winter sale.

97

DON HIGH-END FASHION
AT COLEMAN COLLECTION

Coleman Collection offers first-class service and high-end fashion in downtown Greenville. Founded by Jennifer Coleman, this boutique offers a curated selection of globally sourced clothing, ensuring every piece is as interesting as the woman who wears it. Whether you're searching for chic casualwear, polished career looks, or statement-making evening attire, the staff at Coleman Collection will have plenty of suggestions. They are known for stocking luxury brands like Meimeij, Pinko, Edward Achour Paris, David Lerner, and Manoush. For a more personalized shopping experience, consider booking a private appointment to browse current collections in a one-on-one setting. At Coleman Collection, they say shopping is more than a transaction; it's an experience. From personalized styling to trend-forward separates, the boutique is dedicated to the customer experience. Stop by and discover a wardrobe that speaks chic, effortless style.

1 N Main St., Ste. F, 864-546-1304
coleman-collection.com

BUY VINTAGE
AT OLD SKOOL OUTFITTER

The journey of Old Skool Outfitter began with the shared vision of owners Cy'ree Clarke and Zach Justice: to create a distinct shopping experience utilizing handpicked vintage. After years of running pop-ups and selling online and at markets, the young entrepreneurs opened a brick-and-mortar store on Main Street in downtown Greenville in 2022. Old Skool is a one-stop destination for all things vintage. Their carefully curated collection celebrates timeless pieces and offers a great selection of classic sneakers, throwback jerseys, graphic tees, and memorabilia from iconic rock bands and sports teams. The company operates with a focus on sustainability, emphasizing the importance of reuse and recycling by preserving well-made and historically important pieces of fashion. They believe that vintage fashion is more than just clothing; it's a form of self-expression and makes a statement that bucks trends. Each garment carries a story and a legacy.

123 S Main St., Unit B, 864-236-1983
oldskooloutfitter.com

SAY YES TO THE DRESS
AT THE POINSETT BRIDE

Celebrating 20 years, the Poinsett Bride has been Greenville's premier destination for brides. Just south of Main Street, this elegant boutique offers an inviting atmosphere where every bride—or debutante—will feel confident trying on as many dresses as their heart desires. From classic elegance to modern silhouettes, the Poinsett Bride believes in finding the "just right" dress for each customer. Their expert consultants provide personalized guidance, a stress-free shopping experience, as well as a perfect fit for every gown. As a female-owned business, they understand the personal and cultural significance of wedding planning. The Poinsett Bride celebrates all brides, offering support and encouragement throughout the process. More than just finding a dress, they help create lasting memories that will be cherished for a lifetime.

101C W Court St., 864-241-0730
thepoinsettbride.com

100

TASTE A WORLD OF FLAVOR
AT OIL & VINEGAR

Oil & Vinegar is on the first block of downtown Greenville, right next to NOMA square. We've all been to these types of stores, but this Oil & Vinegar location has chef-owner Veera Gaul at its helm, who not only holds a PhD but was also the provost of Johnson & Wales, the renowned culinary school. The experience here is exceptional, and every employee Veera hires has the chops to help customers make delicious decisions. There are lots of handcrafted culinary gifts, baskets to assemble, and so many oils and vinegars to taste, of course. Veera is also a national buyer for the company, so she is thrilled to share some of her personal favorite things to bring home. There is a curated selection of dishware, books, tools, and prepared foods too. They also host custom events, perfect for groups of friends or team building with coworkers.

220 N Main St., #203, 864-241-6689
oilandvinegarusa.com

ACTIVITIES
BY SEASON

WINTER

Go Coffee Tasting at Coffee Underground and Methodical, 39

Experience the Thrill of the Greenville Swamp Rabbits, 76

Create Your Own Scent at Greenville Soy Candle Company, 117

Make Cocktail Hour a Twofer at Swordfish Cocktail Club and the Rabbit Hole, 3

Brunch at Fork and Plough, 12

Get Some 'Que at Mike & Jeffs, 30

Fall into the World of Jasper Johns at Greenville County's Art Museum, 102

SPRING

Watch Main Street from Above at Jianna, 20

Experience Art in Public Places, 86

Catch a Ball at Fluor Field, 58

Hop on the Swamp Rabbit Trail, 64

Show Your Hometown Pride with the Greenville Triumph, 79

Shop like an Insider at the Wilson Girls Pop-Up, 127

Get Outside at Unity Park, 61

SUMMER

Kick-Start Your Weekend at Saturday Market, 42

Order a Pomegranate Martini at Pomegranate On Main, 6

Snap a Selfie at the Stone Mural Project, 50

Experience Main Street Fridays, 52

Get Your Bard On at Shakespeare in the Park, 55

Pick a Bouquet at Sassafrass Flower Farm, 71

Get Ready to Get Wet at Splash on Main, 132

FALL

Buy a Ticket for Euphoria, 43

Go Where the Galleries Are in West Greenville, 90

Camp at the Albino Skunk Fest, 54

Hike Paris Mountain State Park, 62

Bike like the Pros at Hotel Domestique, 81

Stroll Historic Earle Street, 98

Visit One of the Oldest Buildings in the Upstate at Hans & Franz, 106

Celebrate the Handmade at Indie Craft Parade, 116

SUGGESTED ITINERARIES

FIND YOUR FAVORITE OUTDOOR ACTIVITY

Kick-Start Your Weekend at Saturday Market, 42

Explore Falls Park and the Liberty Bridge, 94

Ride the Trolley Through Downtown, 74

Win a Match at PKL Park, 66

Hop on the Swamp Rabbit Trail, 64

Mountain Bike Gateway Park, 65

Catch a Ball at Fluor Field, 58

EPIC DATE NIGHT

Pick a Bouquet at Sassafrass Flower Farm, 71

Make Cocktail Hour a Twofer at Swordfish Cocktail Club and the Rabbit Hole, 3

Watch a Panoramic Sunset at Juniper, 8

Order It All at Scoundrel, 24

Indulge at Larue Fine Chocolate, 14

GIRLS TRIP

Brunch at Fork and Plough, 12

Get Up Close to Local Artists at Art & Light Gallery, 44

Stroll Historic Earle Street, 98

Snap a Selfie at the Stone Mural Project, 50

Discover Unique Treasures at Urban Digs, 118

Take a Cooking Class at the Cook's Station, 110

Sit at the Chef's Counter at CAMP, 19

GUYS TRIP

Devour a Cathead Biscuit at Maverick, 23

Experience Timeless Style and Unmatched Service at Rush Wilson, 115

Go to the BMW Zentrum, 105

Slurp Oysters at the Jones Oyster Co., 22

Chip Away at 3's Greenville Golf and Grill, 60

Inhale Tacos at Comal 864, 17

Catch a Show at Radio Room, 45

BUNCHES OF FAMILY FUN

Devour Crepes at Tandem, 29

Get Off the Trail at The Commons, 26

Experience an Award-Winning Children's Museum, 88

Experience Art in Public Places, 86

Explore a Secret Garden, 69

Become Part of the Story at M. Judson Booksellers, 124

Get Some 'Que at Mike & Jeffs, 30

ART LOVER'S RETREAT

Visit a Church Full of Artists at Oyé Studios, 91

Go Where the Galleries Are in West Greenville, 90

Take a Cooking Class at the Cook's Station, 110

Fall into the World of Jasper Johns at Greenville County's Art Museum, 102

Shop like an Insider at the Wilson Girls Pop-Up, 127
Find All the Mice on Main, 101
Watch the Documentary *Great Wall* and Then Dine at Sum Bar, 4

THE HISTORY MAVEN

Check Out a Reimagined Textile Complex at the Taylors Mill, 104
Walk Across the Poinsett Bridge, 92
Stand Where the Claussen Bakery Strike Occurred, 84
Order Fried Chicken at OJ's Diner, 32
Climb the Campanile at Furman University, 85
Go to the BMW Zentrum, 105
Visit One of the Oldest Buildings in the Upstate at Hans & Franz, 106

INDEX

Albino Skunk Fest, 54
Art & Light, 44
Art in Public Places, 50, 86
Aryana Afghan Cuisine, 27
Augusta Twenty, 114
Beechwood Farms, 72
BMW Zentrum, 105
Buffington, Ed, 2
CAMP, 19
Campanile (Furman University), 85
Cannada, Geoff (Radio Room), 45
Charles Hedgepath & Friends, 45
Children's Museum of the Upstate, 88
Claussen Bakery Strike, 84
Coleman Collection, 133
Comal 864, 17
Commons, The, 26
Community Tap, The, 2, 26, 119
Cook's Station, The, 71, 110
Coral, 5
Custard Boutique, 126
Drake, David, 103
Drive, The, 5, 58, 59, 74
Drop-In Store, The, 11
Earle Street Historic District, 98
Euphoria, 43
Falls Park and Liberty Bridge, 6, 20, 51, 55, 63, 64, 67, 94, 95, 101, 107, 122
Fireforge Crafted Beer, 10
Fork and Plough, 12
Freeman, Jean Wilson, 36, 50, 127
Furman Golf Club, 78
Gateway Park, 65
Gibson Organic Farms, 42
Grand Bohemian Gallery, 122
Grateful Brew, 34
Greenville County Museum of Art, 102
Greenville Drive, 5, 58, 59, 74
Greenville History Tours, 97
Greenville Swamp Rabbits, 76
Greenville Theatre, 51
Greenville Triumph, 79
Greenville Zoo, 67, 70, 95
Harringtons, 128, 129
Harry's Hoagie Shoppe, 37, 38
Hincapie, George (Hotel Domestique), 81
Hotel Domestique, 81
Hughes Main Library, 51, 89
Indie Craft Parade, 116
Jackson, Shoeless Joe, 59

Jasmine Kitchen, 36
Jianna, 20, 21
Johns, Jasper, 102
Jones Oyster Co., 22
Juniper, 8
Kelly, Shawn (Fork and Plough), 12
LaRue Fine Chocolate, 14, 26
Lazy Goat, The, 25, 48
Linky Stone Park (The Children's Garden), 64, 69
Main Street Fridays, 52
Mast General Store, 101, 130, 131
Maverick Biscuit, 23
Mayar, Nelo (Aryana Afghan Cuisine), 27
McDaniel, Elizabeth Logan (LaRue Fine Chocolate), 14
Methodical Coffee, 26, 39
Mike & Jeffs, 30
M. Judson Booksellers, 101, 124, 125
Mullarkey McGowan, Sunny, 44, 50, 90
Naked Pasta, 42
Nolan, John (Greenville History Tours), 97
Northampton Wine + Dine, 16
O.P. Taylor's, 112
OJ's Diner, 32
Oil & Vinegar Greenville, 136
Okupinksi, Mike (The Community Tap), 2
Old Skool Outfitter, 134
Oyé Studios, 91
Paris Mountain State Park, 62
Paseo, 26
Peace Center, The, 48, 49, 101
Pearlie Harris Mural, 86
Petal Pickers Flower Farm, 120
Pick, Roddy, 12
Pink Bee, 111
PKL Park, 66
Poinsett Bridge, 92, 93
Poinsett Bride, The, 135
Poinsett Hotel, The, 100
Pomegranate On Main, 6
Radio Room, 17, 40, 45
Rabbit Hole, The, 3
Rise Bakery, 35
Rush Wilson Limited, 115
Saturday Market, 42, 72
Scoundrel, 24
Seay, Cathleen Wilson, 127
Shakespeare in the Park, 55, 94
Shoeless Joe Jackson Museum, 59
Simons, Lisa, 28
Smileys on the Roxx, 46
Sobocinski, Carl, 43
Soby's New South Cuisine, 18
Splash on Main, 132
Spivey, Jay (Hans & Franz regular), 106

Stansberry, Bracken (Art & Light), 44
Stone Mural Project, 50
Sum Bar, 4
Sully's Steamers, 33
Swamp Rabbit Cafe & Grocery, 64
Swamp Rabbit Trail, 2, 26, 29, 64, 65, 67, 69
Tandem Crêperie & Coffeehouse, 29
Taylors Mill, The, 104, 116
Triumph, Greenville, 79
Trolley, 74, 75
Turner, Wesley (The Nested Fig), 120
Unity Park, 14, 61, 66, 127
Urban Digs, 118, 119
Van Helten, Guido, 86, 87
Vann & Liv, 129
Walcher, Amy (Urban Digs), 118
Warehouse Theatre, The, 51, 55
Warren, Eli, 44
Well, The (Bon Secours Wellness Arena), 53
West End, 5, 46, 51, 114
Wilson Girls, 126